# Hybrid Judaism

## Irving Greenberg, Encounter, and the Changing Nature of American Jewish Identity

PRESENTED BY

BAY AREA
WEXNER ALUMNI

JCF JEWISH COMMUNITY FEDERATION & ENDOWMENT FUND

## Studies in Orthodox Judaism

**Series Editor: Marc B. Shapiro** (University of Scranton, Scranton, Pennsylvania)

**Editorial Board**

Alan Brill (Seton Hall University, South Orange, New Jersey)
Benjamin Brown (Hebrew University, Jerusalem)
David Ellenson (Hebrew Union College, New York)
Adam S. Ferziger (Bar-Ilan University, Ramat Gan)
Miri Freud-Kandel (University of Oxford, Oxford)
Jeffrey Gurock (Yeshiva University, New York)
Shlomo Tikoshinski (Jerusalem Institute for Israel Studies, Jerusalem)

ACADEMIC
STUDIES
PRESS

# Hybrid Judaism

Irving Greenberg, Encounter, and the
Changing Nature of American
Jewish Identity

DARREN KLEINBERG

Boston
2016

Library of Congress Cataloging-in-Publication Data

**Names:** Kleinberg, Darren, 1976-author.
**Title:** Hybrid Judaism: Irving Greenberg, encounter, and the changing nature of American Jewish identity / Darren Kleinberg.
**Description:** Boston: Academic Studies Press, 2016.
**Series:** Studies in Orthodox Judaism series | Includes bibliographical references and index.
**Identifiers:** LCCN 2016037875 (print) | LCCN 2016040741 (ebook) | ISBN 9781618115454 (hardcover) | ISBN 9781618115461 (e-book)
**Subjects:** LCSH: Greenberg, Irving, 1933- | Rabbis—United States— Biography. | Multiculturalism—Religious aspects—Judaism. | Multiculturalism—United States. | Orthodox Judaism—United States— History—20th century. | Orthodox Judaism—United States— History—21st century. | Judaism—20th century. | Judaism— 21st century. | Judaism—Essence, genius, nature.
**Classification:** LCC BM755.G74 K54 2016 (print) | LCC BM755.G74 (ebook) | DDC 296.8/32092 [B]—dc23 LC record available at https:// lccn.loc.gov/2016037875

ISBN 978-1-61811-545-4 (hardback)
ISBN 978-1-61811-546-1 (electronic)
©Academic Studies Press, 2016

Book design by Kryon Publishing
www.kryonpublishing.com
Cover design by Ivan Grave

Published by Academic Studies Press
28 Montfern Avenue
Brighton, MA 02135, USA
press@academicstudiespress.com
www.academicstudiespress.com

*For Rav Yitz*

# Contents

# Acknowledgments

Although I was not aware of it at the time, this book had its genesis on the evening of May 8, 2003. That was the date on which I first met Irving Greenberg.[1] Toward the end of my second year as a rabbinical student at the fledgling Yeshivat Chovevei Torah in New York City, three optional after-hours sessions were scheduled with Greenberg on the subject of Judaism and Sexuality. I was not familiar with Greenberg, but the fact that these sessions were not part of the regularly scheduled program alerted me to the possibility that he was a controversial figure in the Orthodox world. It was during these sessions that I was exposed to aspects of Greenberg's theology and how he applied it, in this case with regard to intimate relations. At the end of the first session, I shared a taxi back to Riverdale, where Greenberg and I both lived, and began to develop a profoundly important relationship with him. Of the many rabbinic mentors I have had, it is Greenberg alone who has unfailingly embodied his own teachings and values. A man of extraordinary compassion and empathy, matched only by his penetrating intellect, Greenberg remains the most influential mentor in my life to this day. Even as I left Orthodoxy, Greenberg remained an ally and a friend. Thirteen years after that first encounter, I acknowledge the many gifts I have received from Irving Greenberg during that time, not least of all the inspiration to complete this project.

There are a great many others who deserve recognition, without whom this project would never have come to fruition. First and

---

1 Greenberg is known almost universally simply as "Yitz"; however, I have chosen to use his formal name throughout the book.

foremost, I want to thank the good people at Academic Studies Press, who made a dream come true when they invited me to publish with them. Specifically, my thanks go to the Jewish Studies Acquisition Editor, Gregg Stern, and to the editor of the Studies in Orthodox Judaism series, Marc B. Shapiro.

This book is a reworking of my doctoral thesis, which was submitted and defended at the end of 2014. Singular thanks go to my doctoral advisor, Joel Gereboff. In 2009, when Joel was still the Chair of the Religious Studies Department at Arizona State University, he encouraged me to consider applying to graduate school. Despite my lack of an undergraduate degree, Dr. Gereboff worked with me to produce a portfolio and make the case to the graduate admissions department. My sincere thanks go to Arizona State University (Go Devils!) for considering my application and making the highly unorthodox decision to enroll me in the doctoral program in the Religious Studies department.

During my time at ASU, and in addition to Dr. Gereboff, I worked closest with Tracy Fessenden and Moses Moore. My courses with each of them broadened and deepened my understanding of religion in America, and sharpened my focus around questions of pluralism and postethnicity. They ultimately agreed to serve as members of my doctoral committee. I will forever be in their debt for the time and energy they invested in my growth as a student and scholar.

After the completion of my doctorate, I considered the possibility of turning my thesis into a book. I have been blessed with extraordinary friends, colleagues, and mentors who willingly gave of their time to review my thesis and make recommendations. Marc Dollinger and David Ellenson readily agreed to read the entire thesis, providing copious feedback and direction for how to transform my thesis into a book. Their honesty and clarity helped me quickly realize how much work I had ahead of me. In addition, Jack Wertheimer read the thesis chapter that surveyed American Jewish history and saved me from what would have been some rather embarrassing errors. Ari Kelman also took time to read an edited version of the manuscript in toto and presented me with characteristically thoughtful feedback. I feel exceedingly lucky to call each of them colleagues and friends, and am grateful for their time and dedication. Of course, any errors that have remained in the manuscript are utterly my own.

I am additionally thankful to David Ellenson for recommending that I contact Elisheva Urbas to help me reorganize the thesis into a more readable narrative. Elisheva is a gifted editor, who provided critical guidance to generate a more workable outline for the book. Without her input, I am not sure the book would have made it to this point. I also want to thank Eileen Wolfberg for putting the finishing touches on the manuscript to prepare it for publication.

During the summer of 2014, I was lucky enough to be invited to participate in the Oxford Summer Institute in Modern and Contemporary Judaism. For ten days, some of the most respected scholars of Judaism gathered in the idyllic location of Yarnton Manor to consider "Modern Orthodoxy and the Road Not Taken: A Critical Exploration of Questions Arising from the Thought of Rabbi Dr. Irving 'Yitz' Greenberg." The conference presented a unique opportunity to discuss many of the ideas presented in this book and consider many others besides. My thanks go to the conveners, Adam Ferziger and Miri Freud-Kandel, for extending the invitation to participate in the conference. Thanks also go to the other participants: Sylvia Barack Fishman, Steven Bayme, Alan Brill, Arye Edrei, Zev Farber, Michael Fishbane, Martin Goodman, Blu Greenberg, Irving Greenberg, Samuel Heilman, Alan Jotkowitz, Steven Katz, James Kugel, Melissa Raphael, Tamar Ross, Marc Shapiro, Margie Tolstoy, and Jack Wertheimer.

It was at the Oxford gathering that I was lucky enough to meet Aryeh Rubin, a former student of Greenberg's. I am gratified to acknowledge the support of Targum Shlishi, a Raquel and Aryeh Rubin Foundation, for their generous contribution toward the publication of this book.

In many cases, writing a doctoral thesis is a solitary act. For me, I was lucky that a rabbinical school classmate and dear friend was also working toward a PhD, with Greenberg as a research focus. I am thankful to Josh Feigelson for his friendship and his willingness to share ideas freely on a subject about which we both care deeply.

There have also been close friends who have taken an interest in my work and have read drafts of the manuscript and provided valuable feedback. In particular, I want to thank my dear friends Mari Chernow, Aaron Hahn Tapper, Sander Nassan, and Elana Storch for their thoughtful reactions to my work.

Most important of all has been my family. Despite a great many missed Sundays and a few missed vacations, my wife, Debra, and our daughters, Laila and Talia, have supported my efforts without question. Without their willingness to make space for me to do this work, it would never have come to completion. I am not sure it is a debt that can be repaid, but I will certainly try.

I used to think that I was writing this book to explain my world to our daughters. I have recently come to the realization that, in fact, I have been writing it to explain their world to us.

# Preface

It's a challenge to navigate identity. What Israel Zangwill offered as a rather simplistic melting pot metaphor describing how peoples and their cultures integrated into a new composite America developed some years later into Horace Kallen's orchestra, a pluralist approach that celebrated each sound in a way that strengthened the nation for its cultural differences. In contemporary America, neither of those approaches to describing identity pass muster. The melting pot demands the end of distinctiveness since everyone must give up the Old World to become part of the amalgamated new nation. The orchestra, while celebrated in theory, favors the cultural mores of the dominant group at the expense of minorities. To dramatize the point: which ethnic group gets to be the culture-defining tuba in the orchestra and which must be relegated to status as a lowly flute, struggling to have its contribution recognized?

In recent years, scholars have advanced a variety of new models to better understand the contours of identity. "Postethnicity," for example, asks us to look beyond the timetables of the early theorists and imagine identity along a much longer chronology. Others reject the very constructs of identity, describing it all as "the invention of ethnicity." In today's headlines, we read about intersectionality, the notion that each of us lives a variety of identities simultaneously. Sometimes they exist in conflict with one another and at all times our multi-identified selves force us to imagine new ways of understanding and describing who we are, what we believe, and why.

As Darren Kleinberg explains in *Hybrid Judaism: Irving Greenberg, Encounter, and the Changing Nature of American Jewish Identity,* these seemingly secular concepts of identity resonate within the theological and sociological experiences of American Jews. To better articulate models of ethnicity, he argues, we must examine American Judaism as a gateway that offers vital new insights into our sense of individual identity and its impact on larger questions of intergroup relations. For Kleinberg, this exciting new model of ethnic identity grew from the thinking and writing of his mentor, Rabbi Irving Greenberg. "Yitz," as he is known to all, dove into these questions more than half a century ago, fashioning novel understandings of identity that sought to reconcile some of the most challenging identity-based questions in both American and Jewish life. While his work predates the term, Yitz lives an intersectional existence. Greenberg, a tradition-bound Jew with a Ph.D. in history from Harvard University, wrestles with how these different identities intersect, especially in a post-Shoah world. What a remarkable journey it has been.

Greenberg embodies what anthropologists call liminality, an in-between ritual moment during a person's transition from one sociological space to another. Applied more broadly, liminality has also been employed to describe a person who enjoys the rewards of simultaneous membership in more than one cultural group, yet, as a consequence, can never enjoy complete access to either. Greenberg's life journey, then, proves liminal. A modern Orthodox Jew, he cannot enjoy modernity to its fullest extent because of his observance of Jewish law. Complete adherence to traditional Judaism, in a similar way, remains elusive as long as he chooses to interact in the modern world. Many of his teachings, as a consequence, brought scrutiny from his rabbinical colleagues fearful that he went too far. His decision to maintain a primary identity as rabbi precluded an academic career typical of Harvard doctoral graduates.

In that space between Jewish tradition and modern America, in that tension and drama, Greenberg got to work. Liminality, it turns out, offers insights available only to those navigating between cultures. From his platform, Greenberg opined on the essential theological relationship between Judaism and Christianity, on the influence of modern America to the traditional world, on the horrors of the Shoah and its reframe of the cosmos. He can offer these perspectives in ways his predecessors could not *because* he trespassed identity bounds at each and every possible moment.

And so did Kleinberg. A student of Greenberg's, Kleinberg's ode to his mentor grows from his own journey through the spaces between cultures. Born and raised a secular Jew in London, Kleinberg rebelled against the culture of his youth, eschewing the university pathway in favor of a yeshiva experience in Israel that led to a four-year immersion in the tradition-bound Orthodox world of Eretz Yisrael. While the *ba'al teshuvah* pathway is not so unusual, Kleinberg elevated his with his own, sometimes intense, liminal experience. Navigating between a secular upbringing that lacked a passion for Judaism and an adult life in *haredi* and Modern Orthodox Judaism that seemed far too rote, Kleinberg eventually landed as a student in the second-ever graduating class of Yeshivat Chovevei Torah, New York's liberal Orthodox rabbinical school. There, seeking a via media between the cultures that defined his life, Kleinberg met Greenberg, who would emerge as his most-important teacher, mentor, and friend. Greenberg helped shape the contours of Kleinberg's then-emerging theology, understandings of Judaism, and its application in American life. In the years that followed, Kleinberg applied his secular adolescence and impressive understanding of text and tradition to his Greenberg apprenticeship, wrestling with the most essential questions about what Jewishness and Americanness mean.

Kleinberg's journey eventually brought him out of Orthodoxy and, in a fitting reverse parallel to his mentor's path, into his own Ph.D. program at a secular American university. This book, the product of those doctoral studies at Arizona State University, details the life of Yitz Greenberg as it, in its very creation, reflects as well the pathway of his student, Darren Kleinberg. *Hybrid Judaism*, then, when read with an understanding of the story behind its creation, mirrors itself. It is the story of a teacher, an Orthodox Jew who dove into secularity, written by his student, a secular Jew who embraced Jewish tradition.

To read this work, then, is to watch three streams intersect: the life of Greenberg, the life of Kleinberg, and the overlay of the last 50 years of American Jewish life and theology. It is a treat and it offers its readers a deep dive into the most fundamental and the most complex questions that animate all who think about ethnicity, about theology, and about what it means to identify as an American Jew.

**Marc Dollinger**
San Francisco State University

# Introduction

The American Jewish community is changing. In simple terms, Judaism today is but one choice among an almost endless list of available identities. One way of understanding this change is rooted in the writings of the central personality of this study, Rabbi Dr. Irving Greenberg. In 1974, Greenberg presented the opening paper at the International Symposium on the Holocaust, held at the Cathedral of Saint John the Divine, in New York City. The paper was subsequently published in a volume entitled *Auschwitz: Beginning of a New Era? Reflections on the Holocaust* (1977). Greenberg's chapter, "Cloud of Smoke, Pillar of Fire: Judaism, Christianity, and Modernity after the Holocaust," represents his "most important statement on the subject" of the Holocaust (Katz, "Irving," 62). In the fourth section of the essay, addressing "Jewish Theological Responses to the Holocaust," Greenberg introduced his original concept of *Moment Faiths*. Extending Martin Buber's notion of "moment gods,"[1] Greenberg wrote that a full realization of the horrors of the Holocaust had to "end[] the easy dichotomy of atheist/theist ...," and that, in a post-Holocaust age, "We now have to speak of 'moment faiths,' moments when Redeemer and vision of redemption are present, interspersed with times when the flames and smoke of the burning children blot out faith—though it flickers again" (Greenberg, "Cloud of Smoke," 27). In a post-Holocaust era, Greenberg declared, faith in God could only be fleeting.

---

1 Greenberg explained Buber in this way: "God is known only at the moment when Presence and awareness are fused in vital life. This knowledge is interspersed with moments when only natural, self-contained, routine existence is present." (Greenberg, "Cloud of Smoke" 27).

Today, more than 40 years after the symposium, and more than 70 years after the end of the Second World War, American Jews are in a different "moment." Rather than moment gods or moment faiths, the twenty-first-century American Jewish reality is one of *Moment Judaisms*. In this coinage, the plural form "Judaisms" is intended to indicate the very real distinctions between the many different expressions of Judaism across the American Jewish landscape.[2] The sheer variety of Jewish behaviors, rituals, and social mores demands an acknowledgment of the plurality of Jewishness and Judaisms. Furthermore, the simple fact that some will deny that other self-identified Jews are members of the same religious community demands that we cannot but think of Judaism in plural terms.[3]

In addition to highlighting the plurality of contemporary American Jewish life, it is also my contention that contemporary Judaisms are "momentary." The intent here is to recognize the impact of increasingly complex individual and group identities in the American Jewish context. For an increasing number of American Jews, the many Judaisms from which to choose are only some of the various identities that are available for adoption and that contribute to the complex identity politics of postethnic America. David Hollinger has described identity in postethnic America as no longer inherited, singular, or fixed, but rather voluntary, overlapping, and dynamic. As such, postethnicity has very real implications for Jewish identity in the twenty-first century. As Shaul Magid has written, in an era of postethnicity, "... American Jews are multiethnic. For many of them, being Jewish is one part of a more complex narrative of

---

2  The same might be said for world Jewry; however, my work addresses only the American Jewish experience.

3  For example, according to the interpretation of Jewish law (*halachah*) recognized by most members of the Orthodox community, one can only claim Jewish status if one has a halachically Jewish biological mother or if one has completed a religious conversion according to Orthodox standards. As such, those Reform Jews that have a Jewish father and a non-Jewish mother, or that convert to Judaism according to non-Orthodox standards, are not considered Jewish by most members of the Orthodox community. Therefore, it is appropriate to describe the Orthodox and Reform Jewish communities as representing distinct Judaisms.

identity" (Magid, *American Post-Judaism*, 11). These plural and momentary qualities call our attention to the fact that the nature and meaning of American Jewish identity—of American Moment Judaisms—is being renegotiated in the twenty-first century.

Rather than merely attempting to describe the changing nature of American Jewish identity, I will also offer a theological viewpoint that welcomes and embraces, rather than rejects, the changes I will outline. At the heart of this book is an appreciation and exploration of the theological contributions of Irving Greenberg. The postethnic reality that David Hollinger described in sociological terms was powerfully anticipated and conveyed in the language of theology by Greenberg. I have called Greenberg's theology of encounter Hybrid Judaism. Although not a biography, per se, I will also draw on important biographical episodes in Greenberg's life to provide important context for the development and culmination of his theology of Hybrid Judaism. Before fully introducing this concept, it is important to define some key terms.

## Encounter and Identity

Encounter and identity are key terms that are interconnected and require definition. Simply put, encounter refers to interactions that result in a transformation of identity. Such transformations can be the result of encounters with individuals or groups, and sometimes as a result of encounters with ideas or past historical events. As we shall see later,[4] for Greenberg, encounter is also a theological term that refers to interactions that are informed by recognition that human beings are created in the image of God. Whether understood sociologically or theologically, encounter is central to our understanding of the changing landscape of identity.

As David Hollinger has suggested, the word "identity" is less than ideal. In Hollinger's words, "the concept of identity is more

---

4  See Part II, Chapter 9.

psychological than social, and it can hide the extent to which the achievement of identity is a social process by which a person becomes affiliated with one or more acculturating cohorts" (Hollinger, *Postethnic America*, 6). Hollinger's point, that individuals become affiliated with groups (i.e., they adopt identities) as a result of a social process, is of central importance. Throughout this book, the term "identity" is intended to refer to an individual's affiliation, and thus sense of *identification*, with a given group—whether religious, cultural, ethnic, or any other—that results from socialization with that group. This emphasis on affiliation "calls attention to the social dynamics" that are involved in the achievement of identity (Hollinger, *Postethnic America*, 6). As a result, identity may be comprised of multiple affiliations with a variety of social groups. This is a critically important realization in the age of postethnicity.

Regarding the changing nature of American Jewish identity, intermarriage must be acknowledged as the most significant of social encounters contributing to the rise of Moment Judaisms. The Pew survey, *A Portrait of Jewish Americans* (2013), showed that in the 1970s more than a third of the marriages of American Jews were to a non-Jewish spouse and that, since the second half of the 1990s, the percentage had risen to more than half. These couples, and the offspring that are raised by them, have increasingly complex identities that are informed by the various religious, cultural, and ethnic ties that intersect their family lives. Shaul Magid[5] has proposed that

---

5   Magid is the first scholar to pay significant attention to "[American] Judaism in an increasingly postethnic world, a world where identities are mixed ... ... " (Magid, *American Post-Judaism*, 5). In addition to Magid's assessment of American Judaism in an age of postethnicity, he also makes the case for the Jewish Renewal movement and its founding figure, Rabbi Zalman Schachter-Shalomi, as representing a path for "'Jewish' survival in such a shifting society" (Magid, *American Post-Judaism*, 2). While I am generally in agreement with Magid's assessment of the meaning of American Judaism in an age of postethnicity (notwithstanding the distinction I draw above), it is my contention that Irving Greenberg's life and work are more accessible to a broader cross-section of American Jewry than are Schachter-Shalomi's, whose worldview—and the Renewal movement that

the changing nature of Judaism in America "is only partly the consequence of the empirical nature of intermarriage." According to Magid, "It is also the consequence of the changing nature of identity in America, moving from the inherited to the constructed or performed" (Magid, *American Post-Judaism*, 2). In contrast to Magid's claim, I am proposing that the changing nature of identity that he has highlighted is precisely *the result* of increasing social encounters across group lines, with intermarriage being the most significant example. When the influence of high rates of intermarriage is accounted for alongside a wide variety of Jewish beliefs and practices, as well as differing standards for claiming personal status as a Jew, it becomes clear that we need to develop a more thoughtful and nuanced way of thinking about American Jewish identity in the twenty-first century.

## Hybridity

In 2007, the Spertus Museum in Chicago took a step in the right direction when it hosted a groundbreaking exhibit entitled *The New Authentics: Artists of the Post-Jewish Generation*. The accompanying volume opened with an essay from curator Staci Boris, in which she wrote that "*Post-Jewish* ... takes its cues from postmodernism—a pervasive if highly contested state of cultural affairs in which all notions of purity and certainty (modernism's key values) are rejected in favor of hybridity and relativity" (Boris, *The New Authentics*, 20). As the ensuing chapters of this book will demonstrate, it is the quality of hybridity that distinguishes contemporary Moment

followed from it—is appealing to a much more rarefied group. For an important discussion of Magid's book, see Allan Arkush, "All-American, Post-Everything," *Jewish Review of Books*, Fall 2013, https://jewishreviewofbooks.com/articles/473/all-american-post-everything/; Shaul Magid, "'Why Bother?' A Response," *Jewish Review of Books*, August 29, 2013, https://jewishreviewofbooks.com/articles/545/why-bother-a-response/; and Allan Arkush, "'Why Bother?' A Rejoinder," *Jewish Review of Books*, August 29, 2013, http://jewishreviewofbooks.com/articles/543/why-bother-a-rejoinder/.+

Judaisms from earlier articulations of American Jewish identity.[6] "Hybridity" is defined for my purposes as "Anything derived from heterogeneous sources, or composed of different or incongruous elements" (*Oxford English Dictionary* [OED]), and points to the afore-mentioned impact of social mixing on identity formation.[7]

## Pluralism

Pluralism is the final key term that requires definition. In a sense, this book is as much a critique of pluralism as it is anything else. It is my contention that pluralism is an outdated notion that has been superseded by postethnicity. We will explore Horace Kallen's sociological concept of cultural pluralism in detail in Chapter 3 but, for the time being, a few introductory observations are in order.

The earliest usage of the term "pluralism" dates back to the eighteenth century and referred to the simultaneous holding of two or more ecclesiastical offices by one cleric in the Church of England. In this sense, it was seen as a corrupt institution in which "parishes, or benefices, could be bought and sold to the highest bidder" (Bender and Klassen, *After Pluralism*, 7). In addition to this ecclesiastical application, later usages of pluralism have fallen into the philosophical, political, and sociological realms. Philosophically, pluralism has been used to mean "that the world is made up of more than one kind of substance or thing; (more generally) any theory or system of thought which recognizes more than one irreducible basic principle" (*OED*). This philosophical application of

---

6  Other works that have explored the changing nature of American Jewish identity include the wide-ranging collection of essays edited by Vincent Brook, *You Should See Yourself: Jewish Identity in Postmodern American Culture* (2006); Martin Jaffee's collection of short musings, *The End of Jewish Radar: Snapshots of a Postethnic American Judaism* (2009); and Shaul Magid's *American Post-Judaism: Identity and Renewal in a Postethnic Society* (2013).

7  For a more heavily theoretical treatment of hybridity, see Homi K. Bhabha, *The Location of Culture* (1994), and Robert J. C. Young, *Colonial Desire: Hybridity in Theory, Culture, and Race* (1995).

pluralism is most often associated with Harvard philosopher William James (1842–1910) and his 1909 Hibbert Lectures, later published in the volume, *A Pluralistic Universe*. Politically, pluralism has been understood as a "theory or system of devolution and autonomy for organizations and individuals in preference to monolithic state power" or "a political system within which many parties or organizations have access to power" (*OED*). Of these three usages—ecclesiastical, philosophical, and political—the first has largely fallen out of use, with only the philosophical and political senses of pluralism still being employed.[8]

Turning to the sociological meaning of pluralism, the *Oxford English Dictionary* states its fourth definition of pluralism as: "The presence or tolerance of a diversity of ethnic or cultural groups within a society or state; (the advocacy of) toleration or acceptance of the coexistence of differing views, values, cultures, etc." (*OED*). Within this definition are included both descriptive and prescriptive qualities of pluralism. Descriptively, pluralism refers to the simple fact that there is a *plurality*, a diversity, of peoples. Prescriptively, the definition refers to "(the advocacy of) tolerance of a diversity of ethnic or cultural groups within a society or state."[9] While "the presence or tolerance of a diversity of ethnic or cultural groups" is descriptive, "(the advocacy of) tolerance ..." prescribes, in Martin Marty's words, "ways of doing things about the diversities of constituencies ... or ways of thinking about and conceiving them" (Cohen and Numbers, *Gods in America*, x).

---

8 For example, the political scientist, William E. Connolly, has published a philosophical work on the subject of pluralism. See William E. Connolly, *Pluralism* (Durham: Duke University Press, 2005). On the political side see, for example, Thaddeus J. Kozinski, *The Political Problem of Religious Pluralism: And Why Philosophers Can't Solve It* (Lanham: Lexington Books, 2010), and Stephen V. Monsoma and J. Christopher Soper, *The Challenge of Pluralism: Church and State in Five Democracies* (Lanham: Rowman & Littlefield Publishers, Inc., 2009).

9 The questions of who is being tolerated, who is doing the tolerating, and what that means for power dynamics in a given society are important ones. For a thoroughgoing critique of the notion of tolerance, see Wendy Brown, *Regulating Aversion: Tolerance in the Age of Identity and Empire*. (Princeton: Princeton University Press, 2006).

My consideration of pluralism will be limited to its sociological application, paying attention to both descriptive and prescriptive usages of the term. Because the major theorists of pluralism have failed to appreciate the importance of encounter in the achievement of identity, they have also misunderstood the changing nature of identity in America. An appreciation of postethnicity leads to a recognition of the shortcomings of pluralism as a framework with which to understand identity in America in the twenty-first century. Moreover, pluralism is no longer useful if we are to understand the nature of American Jewish identity or navigate the contemporary realities of American Jewish life in the twenty-first century.

## Irving Greenberg and Hybrid Judaism

Irving Greenberg is one of the most influential American Jewish thinkers and activists of the past 50 years. He anticipated the changing nature of contemporary American Jewish identity long before it would become more widely recognized. Until now, much of the scholarship on Greenberg has suffered from an over-emphasis on his work as a Holocaust theologian and as an activist on behalf of Holocaust memory. [10] The result has been that some of his most noteworthy theological and programmatic contributions have passed unnapreciated. Even the most thoughtful treatments of his work have failed to detect how far-reaching his ideas are and the importance they hold for understanding American Jewish identity in the twenty-first century. For Greenberg, the rise of hybrid identities is both a positive and

---

10 See, for example, Steven T. Katz's collection of essays, *Historicism, the Holocaust, and Zionism: Critical Studies in Modern Jewish Thought and History* (1992); Michael L. Morgan's chapter, "Irving Greenberg and the Post-Holocaust Voluntary Covenant," in *Beyond Auschwitz: Post-Holocaust Jewish Thought in America* (2001); and Edward T. Linenthal's *Preserving Memory: The Struggle to Create America's Holocaust Museum* (1995).

necessary development that represents a shift of potentially messianic proportions. Greenberg articulated this understanding through his theology of encounter and his understanding of the evolving nature of the covenant that combine in what I call Hybrid Judaism.

Greenberg's theology of Hybrid Judaism and its emphasis on the power of human encounters can be located along a century-long arc of sociological theories of individual and group identity in America. Beginning with Israel Zangwill's drama of the melting pot and ending with David Hollinger's notion of postethnicity, the greater part of the arc centers around three conceptions of pluralism. Each of these articulations of pluralism—Cultural Pluralism, the Triple Melting Pot, and Multiculturalism—have failed to capture the importance of social dynamics in the achievement of identity, to which David Hollinger has alerted us and to which the realities of contemporary American Jewish life clearly point. Greenberg's work has generally been mischaracterized (by himself as well as others) as advocating pluralism. In actuality, Greenberg's ideas represent a proto-postethnic theology of identity that has much more in common with David Hollinger's work than anyone else along the arc.

Given my emphasis on the importance of social dynamics (encounter) in the formation of identity, it should come as no surprise that Greenberg was himself deeply influenced by a number of profoundly impactful social encounters. As well as receiving great praise for his intellectual and communal efforts, Greenberg has also been publicly criticized by his peers in the Orthodox community, threatened with heresy charges by his rabbinical association, and rejected as an outsider by the centrist Orthodox mainstream and the *haredi* wing of the American Orthodox community. These and other episodes, each of which influenced the formulation of Greenberg's theology of Hybrid Judaism, will be presented throughout the book as evidence in and of themselves of the transformative power of encounter.

## Overview

In order to address the dual purposes of this book—an under-standing of the changing nature of contemporary American Jewish identity and an appreciation of Irving Greenberg's theology of encounter as a way of addressing that reality—it is divided into two parts. Part I introduces Greenberg and examines the broader trends confronting Jewish life in America in particular and religion in America in general. It concludes with an exploration of the century-long arc of sociological theories of identity, culminating with David Hollinger's conception of postethnicity. Part II is devoted to exploring the key encounters in Greenberg's life and the development of his theology of Hybrid Judaism. By presenting these two sections side-by-side, my hope is that the reader will gain a deeper understanding of our contemporary postethnic moment, as well as an appreciation of the opportunity that this new reality presents.

In Chapter 1, I introduce the central figure of this book: Irving Greenberg. By right, Greenberg is one of the most celebrated American Orthodox Jews of the second half of the twentieth century. An ordained rabbi, a Harvard-trained Ph.D., and one of the most influential public figures in American Jewish life, Greenberg was, among a long list of achievements, a founding member of the Association for Jewish Studies, a leading figure in the Christian–Jewish dialogue movement, centrally important to the establishment of the United States Holocaust Memorial Museum, in Washington, DC, and a tireless activist on behalf of intra-Jewish community building. It is my claim that Greenberg was also the earliest American Jewish thought leader to engage notions of postethnicity (although not by that name) head on.

Chapter 1 then turns to American Judaism. Sketching the major contours of the history of the American Jewish community serves to provide the necessary background and context with which to understand the reality into which Greenberg was born and raised. Because so much of Greenberg's work involved attempts to overcome intra-Jewish division, this section is organized primarily around the rise of denominational Judaism in the United States and the accompanying tensions that have plagued the American Jewish community. The chapter concludes with examples of the challenges that confronted American Jewish institutions as they attempted to respond to the increasingly fractious community that they served.

Chapter 2 presents a survey of the historiographical record of American religious history. The historiographical lens serves to narrate the changing understanding—and reality, to be sure—of religion in America. It also highlights the relatively recent emphasis on pluralism by scholars of religion in America and the very real limitations of such an approach if we are to gain an accurate understanding of contemporary American religious diversity.

Chapters 3 and 4 turn our attention to a discussion of the century-long arc of sociological theories of group life in America. By pursuing the shift from the melting pot to postethnicity, it is possible to arrive at a clear understanding of pluralism as a sociological theory that originated with the work of Horace Kallen. Milton Gordon's important critique of Kallen provides the bridge from cultural pluralism to David Hollinger's notion of postethnicity. Gordon's appreciation of the importance of social contact between primary relationships provides the basis for my emphasis on the notion of encounter, a concept central to Greenberg's work. Ultimately, the arc provides a theoretical framework with which to understand the full extent of Irving Greenberg's theology of Hybrid Judaism.

Part II turns our attention to the life and work of Irving Greenberg. By weaving a tapestry of personal encounters and theological insights, the chapters in Part II map the development of Greenberg's thinking, culminating in his theology of Hybrid Judaism. Taken together, the chapters in Part II represent the first complete and systematic presentation of Greenberg's theology of Hybrid Judaism. Although Greenberg himself adopted the language of pluralism, it is clear that his ideas extend beyond pluralism, embracing notions of religious identity that are immediately recognizable as precursors and parallels to Hollinger's conception of postethnicity. Greenberg's notion of Hybrid Judaism describes those Jews who are deeply rooted in their Jewish identity but are also radically open to opportunities for hybridity. Hybrid Judaism affirmatively acknowledges the reality that different expressions of Judaism (including, but not limited to, denominational ones) are influenced, transformed, and—in some cases—coupled with other religious (and ethnic and cultural) identities. Hybrid Judaism has no outer limit and communicates the ability of contemporary expressions of American Moment Judaisms to incorporate any new attachment or affiliation from within or beyond the Jewish context. The full implications of Greenberg's theology of Hybrid Judaism serve to reassert his importance and shed new light on the relevance of his work for our understanding of American Jewish identities in the twenty-first century.

# PART 1

# CHAPTER 1

# Irving Greenberg and the Changing American Jewish Landscape

Placed against the backdrop of twentieth-century American Judaism in particular and religion in America in general, Irving Greenberg is best understood as both of and ahead of his time. His theological response to the changing American and Jewish realities that surrounded him both anticipated and welcomed developments that would have a defining impact on American Jewish life in the twenty-first century. The source of his openness to the changes that would take place around him can be located in a number of key encounters during his formative years.

Born on May 16, 1933, Irving Greenberg was raised in Borough Park, Brooklyn.[1] The American Jewish reality that Greenberg was born into was one of great upheaval and transformation. In 1930, the Jewish population of New York was estimated at more than 1.8 million inhabitants, with Borough Park alone numbering 61,000 Jewish residents (Horowitz and Kaplan, *Jewish Population of the New York Area*, 32). Greenberg was raised with "more learning and piety ... than in the average Jewish home" (Freedman, *Living in the Image of God*, 1) and, unlike many immigrant Jewish families that abandoned the religious commitments of their European forebears, his family remained steadfast. Nonetheless, Greenberg's birth did present his parents with a cultural conflict. Greenberg recalled that,

> when [my father] and my mother came to name their son
> they could not bear the thought that I should be stigmatized

---

1 Also commonly spelled Boro Park.

with a name like Yitzchak, which could label their son as outside the mainstream of American life. So they looked around for the most white Anglo-Saxon, Protestant name they could find, and they found it: Irving! (Greenberg, "End of Emancipation," 48)

Unwilling to hold their son back from the opportunities that America presented, Greenberg's parents opted for a thoroughly American name. By naming their son Irving, the Greenbergs conceded to the new American reality in which they found themselves. Although the younger Greenberg would later embrace a more distinctively Jewish name—"Yitz"—he would continue to confront the tension between his particular identity as a Jew and his embrace of a more open and postethnic identity.

From a young age, Greenberg was exposed to a world outside of his own. The most significant encounter with non-Orthodox Judaism during his childhood years occurred in the company of his father, Rabbi Elias Henry Greenberg (1894–1975). The senior Greenberg was a former student of Rabbi Haim Soloveitchik (1853–1918)[2] and a scholar in his own right. As Greenberg recalled: "The learning was supplied by my father, who was a *talmid chacham*[3] of awesome proportions … He taught Talmud daily in an immigrant congregation" (Freedman, *Living in the Image of God*, 1). Nevertheless, he was also willing to expose his son to a Jewish world beyond just their own. Greenberg recalled this story:

When I look back, certain amazing little experiences stand out. There was one Conservative congregation in Boro Park—Temple Emanuel. David Koussevitsky was *chazzan* there. Many times, on the way back from Beth El (my father's *shul*), my father would take me in to hear Koussevitsky.

---

2 Haim Soloveitchik was the grandfather of Rabbi Joseph B. Soloveitchik, who would become an important influence on the younger Greenberg.

3 Literally, "a wise student." This traditional honorific is used to describe great scholars.

I do not think there were many other Orthodox rabbis from Boro Park who would have gone into that *shul* ... going into a Conservative congregation was not standard operating procedure. By such simple, almost elementary gestures (not only taking me inside to hear the *chazzan*, but also showing respect for the service), he taught me an instinctive pluralism. (Freedman, *Living in the Image of God*, 4)

Greenberg's exposure both to Conservative Judaism and his father's respect for it took place at an early, formative age and left a strong impression.

In another reminiscence, this time of a story he had heard about an episode involving his older sister in 1929 or 1930, Greenberg recalled,

... my sister Lillian walked by a Catholic parochial school located near my parents' apartment around 62nd St. on the border of Borough Park and Bensonhurst. A few of the students apparently harassed her ... The verbal harassment included anti-Semitic slurs. When she came home, she told my father. Instead of letting this go by, my father took her hand and marched her back to the school. He went in and asked to meet with the principal who was a Catholic priest ... the two of them communicated what happened, the fact that they were immigrants, and the fact that my father was a Rabbi. The principal listened respectfully. He then apologized for the boys' behavior. Moreover he called an assembly ... He spoke to [the students] and explained that these were immigrants who had come to America seeking a better life. Therefore Americans should welcome them and treat them with respect and kindness. He also told the boys that my father was a Rabbi and that it was wrong to attack a Rabbi or his child with anti-Semitic slurs ...

The lesson was clear and powerful:

> ... my father told me the story and drew the moral from it. America was different. He said to me that in Poland the clergy themselves would have been anti-Semitic and would encourage such behaviors. He knew or had understood that in America, Christians i.e. Catholics were different. Not only could you assume that they were against anti-Semitic behavior but that one could turn to them for justice. Looking back I believe such a story sowed the seeds of my more positive attitude toward Christianity—seeds that blossomed when I became involved in Jewish Christian dialogue after the Holocaust.[4]

Greenberg's father modeled what it meant to learn from encounters with both non-Orthodox Jews and non-Jews alike.

These vignettes are reminiscent of the paternal influence on another significant American Jewish figure, Mordecai M. Kaplan. Also a devoutly Orthodox rabbi, the older Kaplan exhibited an openness that strongly influenced his son. As Kaplan's biographer has recorded, "Old Rabbi Kaplan was a tolerant man, and frequently the boys were entertained by the conversation of a rather heretical Bible scholar named Arnold Ehrlich ... thus, at an early age, young Mordecai was exposed to Biblical criticism and the problems raised by a scientific study of the Bible" (Scult, *Communings of the Spirit*, 46). For both Kaplan and Greenberg, their fathers opened their eyes to different possibilities at a very young age.[5] While it is impossible to demonstrate the direct influence of these experiences on their later contributions, the impact on Kaplan and Greenberg's development is beyond doubt.

As a child, Greenberg attended Yeshivat Etz Chaim elementary school and then Yeshiva University High School. Both institutions

---

4 Personal e-mail communication, May 26, 2013.
5 Kaplan dedicated his magnum opus, *Judaism as a Civilization* (1934), to his father and credited him with being his "eyes as I wandered in the desert of confusion" (Exodus 14:3).

were located in Brooklyn and both were "in the upper range of Modern Orthodox education in America" (Freedman, *Living in the Image of God*, 1). Following high school, Greenberg attended both Brooklyn College and Beth Joseph Rabbinical Seminary[6] simultaneously. While attending Brooklyn College, and under the influence of his older sister, Lillian, Greenberg became interested in the study of history.

Meanwhile, at Beth Joseph, he was exposed to a particular strain of the Jewish *Musar* tradition of self-improvement that was established in the nineteenth century by Israel Lipkin (1810–1883), popularly known as Yisrael Salanter.[7] Beth Joseph was heir to a branch of the *Musar* tradition that originated in the Eastern European city of Novardok (Navahrudak), which emphasized the negation of the ego and of material desires as a path to the divine. Greenberg has described his experience at Beth Joseph in this way: "Thanks to ... its strong *musar* component, Bais Yosef gave me a dynamic and very different, more moving religious experience ..." (Freedman, *Living in the Image of God*, 3). Taken together with the experience at Brooklyn College, Greenberg has observed that, compared to what his experience might have been had he attended the more Americanized, Modern Orthodox, Yeshiva University, where he could have received both a secular and religious education, his "religious education was much less filtered by modernity, and my college experience ... was much less filtered by Orthodoxy" (Freedman, *Living in the Image of God*, 3). His unadulterated encounter with both the academy and the piety of the *Musar* tradition provided Greenberg with two different perspectives on the world—one through secular scholarship and the other through deep religiosity.

Subsequent to his graduation from Brooklyn College, where he majored in history, and his ordination as a rabbi from Beth Joseph, both in 1953, Greenberg went on to graduate school at Harvard

---

6 Also known as Yeshiva Bais Yosef, or Novardok.

7 Lipkin was known by the name Salanter in recognition of the Lithuanian city (Salantai) where he studied and was mentored by the spiritual father of the *Musar* movement, Rabbi Zundel of Salant (1786–1866).

University. According to Greenberg, his pursuit of rabbinical ordination was intended "simply to please [his] parents, especially [his] father" (Freedman, *Living in the Image of God*, 6). His true intentions remained firmly focused on becoming a secular academician.

Having left the familiar surroundings of Brooklyn, Greenberg now had to navigate the secular world of an elite American college campus. In doing so, Greenberg had to reconsider his custom of always wearing a *kippah*. "The classic example: when I arrived, no one told me, but I just knew that you could not wear a *kippah* … So I wore a hat and took it off when I went into class. As soon as I came out of class, I would put the hat on again." (Freedman, *Living in the Image of God*, 7). Unhappy with this compromise, and in defiance of the unspoken expectation, Greenberg decided to go ahead and don his *kippah* at all times. According to him, "That coming-out was a key transition for me. By then, I was looking to emotionally connect with and serve Jews" (Freedman, *Living in the Image of God*, 7). During this time, and while still a student at Harvard working on his dissertation,[8] Greenberg served as the Rabbi of the Young Israel synagogue in Brookline, Massachusetts, from 1954 to 1955. After completing his studies and receiving his doctorate in American History in 1960, Greenberg pursued a faculty position at Yeshiva University instead of staying at Harvard for a postdoctoral position, and began what would be a lifelong commitment to Jewish education and the Jewish community.

These early encounters exposed Greenberg to the realities of being Jewish in the United States in the twentieth century. He quickly became aware of the challenge of being both Jewish and American at the same time. The dual realities of his parents' Orthodoxy and his American name; Brooklyn College and Beth Joseph; Harvard Yard and his decision to literally wear his Judaism for all to see, set Greenberg on a unique path. Of course, Greenberg was not alone in having to negotiate the challenges of being an American Jew in

---

8 Greenberg's advisor was Frederick Merk (1887–1977), an American historian who taught at Harvard University from 1924 until 1956. The title of Greenberg's dissertation was *Theodore Roosevelt and Labor: 1900–1918*.

the twentieth century. In fact, his reality was rather typical for first-generation-born children of immigrant families trying to find their way in America. But, as I will show, it was his response—informed by the formative example set by his father—that distinguished him from his peers.

Greenberg was raised and came of age at a time when American Judaism was undergoing significant change. From the colonial period up until the second half of the nineteenth century, the Jewish community in America was tiny. It was not until the middle of the nineteenth century that the American Jewish population totaled more than 50,000 members. The earliest American Jews were diverse and "a full gamut of religious observances and attitudes could be found, from deep piety to total indifference" (Sarna, *American Judaism*, 22). By 1860, there were as many as 200,000 Jews living in the United States; beginning in 1880, increasing numbers of European Jewish immigrants arrived on American shores and contributed to the rapid growth of the American Jewish community. Consequently, by the turn of the twentieth century, the population of the American Jewish community had reached more than 1 million members. By 1920, the number was more than 3.5 million (Sarna, *American Judaism*, 375). A rapidly growing American Jewish community meant that, already by the middle of the nineteenth century, religious leaders were lobbying to attract a following for what was, at the time, a fledgling American Jewish denominationalism.[9]

In 1854, Rabbi Isaac Mayer Wise established himself in Cincinnati, Ohio, and, in time, became a major organizer of the American Reform movement. The relationship between the fast-growing Reform movement and the nascent American Orthodox community was tense. In an effort to ameliorate growing tensions, a national conference was called in 1855 by Wise and his Orthodox counterpart, Isaac Leeser,[10] to discuss "a common liturgy, and a plan

---

9  Jewish denominationalism first appeared in the second decade of the nineteenth century with the rise of early Reform Judaism in Germany.

10  Isaac Leeser (1806–1868) was a German-born traditional Jew who arrived in America in 1824. He served as the cantor of Congregation Mikveh Israel of

for promoting Jewish education" (Sarna, *American Judaism*, 108). The response was that "both Wise and Leeser met with enormous criticism." The recently arrived Reform ideologue, Rabbi David Einhorn, "opposed compromises with Orthodoxy on principal," while at the same time "... the Orthodox side ... boycotted the meeting" (Sarna, *American Judaism*, 110). As a result, "Like so many other attempts at compromise in the middle decades of the nineteenth century, this one too failed to take hold" (Sarna, *American Judaism*, 109).[11]

The American Reform movement grew steadily in the nineteenth century as it actively embraced the new era. The construction of Moorish-style, cathedral-like synagogues in major Jewish centers such as Boston, Philadelphia, and New York; the incorporation of organs and choirs to accompany the prayer services; the introduction of family pews; and the production of a new Reform liturgy all contributed to "underscore[] Reform Judaism's break with the past" and served

> (1) to attract younger, Americanized Jews to the synagogue; (2) to make non-Jewish friends and visitors feel welcome; (3) to improve Judaism's public image; and (4) to create the kind of solemn, formal, awe-inspiring atmosphere that high-minded Jews and Christians alike during this period considered conducive to moral reflection and effective devotional prayer. (Sarna, *American Judaism*, 125–126)

---

Philadelphia, was the founding editor of the influential Jewish periodical, *The Occident*, and established the first Jewish Publication Society of America, among numerous other communal roles.

11  Leeser was at the center of prior attempts at unity. In 1841, he developed a "plan for establishing a religious union among the Israelites of America" that would include a Central Religious Council, a network of Jewish schools, and a union of congregational delegates. Shortly afterward, Leeser championed the idea of installing a Chief Rabbi, along the line of the Anglo-Jewish community. Neither of these attempts proved successful (Sarna, *American Judaism*, 103–134).

Furthermore, the establishment of the Union of American Hebrew Congregations in 1873 and the Hebrew Union College in 1875, both in Cincinnati, provided both an organizational arm for the movement and a training ground for new American Reform rabbis. As Jonathan Sarna has noted, by the close of the nineteenth century "Reform Jewish leaders concluded that the cause to which they had devoted their lives had triumphed" (Sarna, *American Judaism*, 129).

Although the Reform movement experienced rapid and dramatic growth throughout the nineteenth century, the demographic landscape began to shift quickly with the growing waves of immigration. The arrival of more than 2 million Eastern European Jews between the early 1880s and 1920s significantly influenced the demographic balance from colonial Jews and their descendants to immigrant Jews from Eastern Europe and Russia. Although only a minority of these new immigrants were "synagogued," they were a sizable group, numbering in the hundreds of thousands. Then, beginning in the 1930s, a cadre of influential Orthodox leaders arrived on American shores. Among them were Rabbi Joseph B. Soloveitchik[12] (arrived in 1932), Rabbi Moshe Feinstein[13] (arrived in 1936), Rabbi Aaron Kotler[14] (arrived in 1941), and Rabbi Menachem Mendel Schneerson[15]

---

12  Soloveitchik (1903–1993), a European-trained Talmudic scholar, philosopher, and theologian, served for over 40 years as the senior Rosh Yeshiva of the Rabbi Isaac Elchanan Theological Seminary (RIETS) and occupied the Lieb Merkin Distinguished Professorial Chair in Talmud and Jewish Philosophy at Yeshiva University, New York. He became the most significant twentieth-century Modern Orthodox leader in the American Jewish community, ordaining some 2,000 rabbis during his tenure.

13  Feinstein (1895–1986), an Orthodox scholar from Lithuania, would become one of, if not the, most influential Jewish-legal decisor of the twentieth century. He served as the head of Mesivtha Tifereth Jerusalem, on the Lower East Side of Manhattan, and was president of the Union of Orthodox Rabbis of the USA and Canada as well as the Moetzes Gedolei Torah of Agudath Israel of America.

14  Kotler (1891–1962) established the Beth Medrash Govoha in Lakewood, New Jersey. It would become one of the largest *yeshivot* (Talmudic seminaries) in the world, serving the *haredi* community.

15  Schneerson (1902–1994) would become the leader of the Chabad-Lubavitch sect of Hasidic Orthodoxy. Under his leadership, the sect would embark on the largest

(arrived in 1941). As a result, the Orthodox community began to assert itself on the American Jewish landscape.

Parallel to the growth of Orthodoxy was the rising influence of Conservative Judaism in the American Jewish community.[16] In 1886, the Jewish Theological Seminary of America (JTS) was established to "steer a course between 'stupid Orthodox and insane Reform'" (Diner, "Like the Antelope and the Badger," 6).[17] Their concern was that the Orthodox and Reform movements "threatened Judaism in America, because both staked out extreme positions and forced Jews to choose sides" (Diner, "Like the Antelope and the Badger," 6). JTS, the flagship institution of American Conservative Judaism, was conceived to train traditional rabbis for a modern American Jewry "thanks largely to Americanizing East European Jews and their children" (Sarna, *American Judaism*, 213).[18] By the middle of the twentieth century, Conservative Judaism had distinguished itself from Reform and Orthodox expressions of Judaism, and became the largest denomination in the American Jewish community (Wertheimer, "Recent Trends," 67).

In addition to these developments, the increasingly influential role of Mordecai M. Kaplan (1881–1983) and his American-born Reconstructionist movement added to the twentieth-century profile of American Judaism. Reconstructionist Judaism presented an alternative, albeit a much smaller one, to the assumed tri-choice of Conservative, Orthodox, and Reform Judaism. More important, as an influential faculty member at JTS and a noted Jewish intellectual for more than half a century, Kaplan exerted a powerful influence over

---

intra-Jewish missionary campaign in Jewish history.

16  American Conservative Judaism was the successor to the Positive-Historical school established by Zecharias Frankel (1801–1875) in Germany after his split from the early Reformers in 1845.

17  Quoted by Diner from an 1895 edition of the periodical, *American Hebrew*.

18  From the time of the establishment of the Seminary until the middle part of the twentieth century, Conservative Judaism did not consider itself, nor was it generally treated as, a separate denomination from, albeit a more modern version of, Orthodox Judaism.

more than a generation of Conservative and Reform rabbis who remained attached to their movements, but were strongly attracted to his ideas.

Kaplan's influence, and the extent to which denominational tensions flared within the American Jewish community, can be illustrated by a disturbing episode. By the middle of the twentieth century, Kaplan was already well established as the most controversial figure in the American Jewish community. Deemed a heretic by many in the Conservative movement and even more so within Orthodoxy, Kaplan was a radical theologian, scholar, and social theorist.[19] In 1945, the Reconstructionist movement published a Sabbath prayer book "which reflected Kaplan's rejection of chosenness. It also removed all references to the idea of the resurrection of the dead and the inevitable coming of the messiah" (Diner, *The Jews of the United States*, 255). Each one of these theological innovations would have been shocking to traditional Jewish ears and eyes by themselves; presented together, they were perceived as a threat that needed to be countered.[20] Even more shocking, though, was the public burning of the prayer book.[21] This act was especially disturbing given that it occurred so soon after the Holocaust, when the burning of Jewish books was a regular form of Nazi terror. This is but one,

---

19  See Jeffrey S. Gurock and Jacob J. Schachter, eds., *A Modern Heretic and a Traditional Community: Mordecai M. Kaplan, Orthodoxy, and American Judaism* (New York: Columbia University Press, 1997).

20  Of course, each of these theological innovations had already been adopted by nineteenth-century Reform Jews in Germany and the United States. The particularly harsh reaction to Kaplan was likely influenced by his own familial and professional ties to the Orthodox community—in addition to being raised in the home of an Orthodox rabbi, Kaplan himself was ordained in Europe by the Orthodox Zionist leader, Rabbi Isaac Jacob Reines and, early on in his career, filled rabbinic posts at the Orthodox Congregation Kehilath Jeshurun and the Jewish Center, in New York City.

21  They also "issued a *herem*, a ban of excommunication against Kaplan" (Diner, *The Jews of the United States*, 255). For a discussion of exactly who was responsible for the book burning, see this blog post from Marc B. Shapiro: http://seforim.blogspot.com/2014/09/r-isaac-arama-r-kook-mordecai-kaplan.html

albeit extreme, example of how fraught relationships were between different religious branches of the American Jewish community.

In the second half of the twentieth century, the rise of the Havurah movement, Jewish Renewal, Neo-Hasidism, Secular Humanistic Judaism, and a number of other groups would further diversify the American Jewish landscape. By the end of the twentieth century, the institutional and numeric strength that Conservative Judaism had exhibited since mid-century would eventually wane while Reform Judaism remained numerically strong and Orthodoxy continued to grow and become more strident.

As has been widely noted, the broader American religious landscape experienced a "slide to the right" in the last third of the twentieth century. This shift was exhibited most powerfully by the numerical and cultural resurgence of an Evangelical Conservatism that would actively challenge the cultural hegemony of more liberal expressions of American Protestantism. A similar movement can be detected in the American Orthodox Jewish community, and has been given its fullest treatment in Samuel Heilman's book, *Sliding to the Right: The Contest for the Future of American Jewish Orthodoxy* (2006).

Heilman posited that the American Orthodox community can be divided into two core groups: pluralist and enclavist.[22] Pluralist Orthodox Jews have "the ability to live in and be embraced by several cultures and worldviews at once" (Heilman, *Sliding to the Right*, 3), whereas enclavist Orthodox Jews "view[] the surrounding modern world not as an opportunity but as a threat and seek[] instead to keep it at arm's length ..." (Heilman, *Sliding to the Right*, 4). For enclavist Orthodox Jews, the need for a mechanism with which to negotiate diversity is less important; after all, they limit their exposure to more progressive Orthodox Jews, non-Orthodox Jews, and non-Jews as much as possible. As Heilman has pointed out, enclavists choose "separation or exclusion [and] create powerful boundaries between those who share their outlook and behavior and those who do not."

---

22 He also acknowledged a third group of Orthodox Jews of Middle-Eastern descent that was not considered due to their limited role in American Orthodox life, as contrasted with Israel.

Furthermore, "[i]n their chosen insularity, they reject the ideal of the melting pot and mobility . . . allowing almost no room for acceptance of cultural pluralism, in which other ways of living can be viewed as legitimate or appropriate for Jews" (Heilman, *Sliding to the Right,* 83). According to Heilman, this has been increasingly the trend in the American Orthodox community. Although some have argued that Orthodoxy is also experiencing its own internal diversification of sorts,[23] Heilman has certainly identified the dominant trend within that community. During this time, the *haredi* (enclavist) Orthodox community has experienced rapid growth while Modern Orthodoxy (pluralist) has seen a steep decline.[24]

The changes taking place on the denominational landscape since the middle of the nineteenth century meant that American Judaism was becoming increasingly fractured. As a result, nonsectarian American Jewish organizations grappled with the challenge of serving a changing American Jewry, with varying levels of success. Different organizations had different responses to the rising denominationalism in American Jewish life. Some attempted to ignore it, while others confronted it head on. What follows is a brief overview of the work of four American Jewish organizations—B'nai B'rith, The Jewish Welfare Board, Hillel, and The Synagogue Council of America—to highlight some of the challenges and limitations of working in this new American Jewish context.

---

23  See Adam S. Ferziger, "Church/Sect Theory and American Orthodoxy Reconsidered," in *Ambivalent Jew: Charles Liebman in Memorium,* ed. Stuart Cohen and Bernard Susser (New York: The Jewish Theological Seminary of America, 2007): 107–123; Adam S. Ferziger, *Beyond Sectarianism: The Realignment of American Orthodox Judaism* (Detroit: Wayne State University Press, 2015); and Yehuda Turetsky and Chaim I. Waxman, "Sliding to the Left? Contemporary American Orthodoxy," *Modern Judaism* 31, no. 2 (May 2011).

24  As Jack Wertheimer wrote in 2014: "Just a few decades ago, the modern sector constituted the large majority of Orthodox Jews; in our time, it has become vastly outnumbered by the Orthodox resisters and is on track to decline even further. As compared with the 3 percent of American Jews who (according to Pew) identify themselves as Modern Orthodox, 6 percent identify themselves as *haredi.* In absolute numbers this translates into an estimated 310,000 adult *haredim* compared with 168,000 adult Modern Orthodox." See Jack Wertheimer, "Can Modern Orthodoxy Survive?" *Mosaic.* http://mosaicmagazine.com/essay/2014/08/can-modern-orthodoxy-survive/

One early American Jewish organization attempted to simply sidestep denominational politics, rather than attempt to navigate the religious tensions of American Jewish life. B'nai B'rith, founded in 1843 as a fraternal order, was a Jewish establishment organization that, according to its historian, Deborah Dash Moore, identified two central areas of focus: "the quest for leadership [of the American Jewish community] and for unity of American Jews" (D. Moore, *B'nai B'rith*, xii). In trying to achieve these goals, the early leaders of B'nai B'rith realized that "[t]he debates between the nascent Reform and Orthodox partisans filled Jewish gatherings with bitterness" and therefore "they would have to avoid religious issues in order to succeed" (D. Moore, *B'nai B'rith*, 4). Consequently, "... B'nai B'rith's founders intended to 'banish from its deliberations all doctrinal and dogmatic discussions,' and framed their rituals 'to be equally unobjectionable to the Orthodox as to the Reformers'" (D. Moore, *B'nai B'rith*, 10). The result was a "pragmatic nonsectarianism" (D. Moore, *B'nai B'rith*, 10) that chose to sidestep denominations and the growing tensions between them.

By contrast, the Jewish Welfare Board (JWB), an early twentieth-century American Jewish organization, sought to incorporate the various denominations in its work. The JWB was organized out of the practical necessity of having a single group that would represent the American Jewish community before the United States government in the latter's attempt to provide for the religious needs of troops in the U.S. Armed Forces. Impressively, the JWB's inaugural meeting in 1917 included "representatives from the five most prominent rabbinical and congregational organizations, the United Synagogue [Conservative], the Union of American Hebrew Congregations [Reform], the Union of Orthodox Jewish Congregations, the Agudath Ha-Rabbonim [Orthodox], and the CCAR [Central Conference of American Rabbis, Reform], together with the Jewish Publication Society" (Cooperman, "A Little Army Discipline," 82). As a result, the JWB did have some success, in no small part due to the involvement of the United States government and the overriding need to provide for Jewish troops.

Despite the laudable efforts of the JWB to "chart a path between Orthodoxy and Reform, hoping that the Judaism that emerged could satisfy and unite Jews from across the religious spectrum" there was still "resistance from both Orthodox and Reform Jews uninterested in finding a compromise position between them" (Cooperman, "A Little Army Discipline," 296–297). In the end, the JWB lost much of its purpose after the end of the First World War. As its historian has noted, "The board's ability to represent all of American Jewry had always derived from its government contract rather than popular consensus" (Cooperman, "A Little Army Discipline," 298). Subsequently, the JWB joined forces with the Young Men's Hebrew Association and turned its focus from serving troops overseas to Jewish communities in the United States.

One of the most tangible examples of the JWB's cross-denominational efforts was its prayer book. Originally published in 1917 under the title *Abridged Prayer Book for Jews in the Army and Navy of the United States*, the prayer book did manage to "introduce soldiers to diverse liturgies and to modes of Jewish worship that some had never before encountered." Despite the fact that "the Orthodox found the final product inappropriately short and the Reform complained that it did 'not reflect our particular theology'" (Sarna, *American Judaism*, 213), the prayer book continued to be produced. A 1984 edition includes thanks to the Central Conference of Reform Rabbis, the Rabbinical Assembly (Conservative), and the Rabbinical Council of America (Orthodox) "for the use and adaptation of their respective liturgical texts," and acknowledges rabbis from each of the three denominations. It is noteworthy that the introduction states that the prayer book "is intended exclusively for use by Jewish personnel in the Armed Forces" and the preface adds that it "is not intended for the general use of those in the civilian community." The preface goes on to reason that "its shortened and compact form is designed specifically for military use." One cannot avoid reading between the lines that this kind of cross-denominational prayer book was only intended to be used "in fox-holes," as it were. As such, and although the JWB did play an important role in serving the needs of Jewish troops in the American Armed Forces, its impact on the broader American Jewish denominational landscape was rather limited.

As already mentioned, B'nai B'rith wished to avoid religious issues whenever possible. Despite this, one American Jewish organization that was founded under its auspices did have some success in addressing the religious diversity of the American Jewish community. In 1923, Rabbi Benjamin Frankel established a new organization that was intended to serve the Jewish student body at the University of Illinois at Urbana-Champaign. Frankel called the organization Hillel which, in the words of one historian, "symbolized learning, tolerance, dignity, courage; Hillel, the first-century sage, a lover of learning, zealous for Jewish life, a gentle and tolerant man who bravely stood up for his convictions, was 'indisputably ... the ideal symbol of the Jewish spirit'" (D. Moore, *B'nai B'rith*, 140). Among other activities, Frankel "conducted Reform services on Friday night [and] Orthodox services on Saturday" (D. Moore, *B'nai B'rith*, 138). Replicating this model across the country, Hillel would become the largest campus-based organization in the American Jewish community. According to Frankel's vision, "Hillel differed in being a nonsectarian Jewish religious organization—that is, it served young Jews from Reform to Orthodox" (D. Moore, *B'nai B'rith*, 139–140). As a result of this approach, Hillel may well have been the most successful American Jewish organization to commit to a sustained program of Jewish engagement across the denominations. Nevertheless, and despite its continued success, in recent decades there has been an increase in sectarian denominationalism on college campuses that has challenged the model of cooperation championed and exemplified by Hillel. The rising number of Chabad houses, other Orthodox Jewish outreach programs, and, in some cases, the hiring of multiple rabbis at a single Hillel center to serve each denominational community raises questions about the extent to which meaningful cross-denominational encounters are actually taking place anymore on college campuses.

A final example of an institutional attempt to bridge the divide between American Jewish denominations is the Synagogue Council of America (SCA). Founded in 1926, the SCA was established in part as an attempt to ensure greater harmony across the leadership of the three major denominations. Paralleling the National Council of Churches, the SCA was intended to provide a central religious address for the American Jewish community that included representatives of the Conservative, Orthodox, and Reform movements. It is notable that at no point in its history were representatives of any other denominations invited or permitted to join. Thus, as Jonathan Golden has pointed out, despite its positive expression of communal unity and institutional solidarity, "it never embraced diversity as a value in itself" (Golden, "From Cooperation to Confrontation," 142).

While the immediate members of the Council did interact with each other, they "created a top down organization without fully developing a natural grassroots following" (Golden, "From Cooperation to Confrontation," 142), thus limiting its impact on the larger American Jewish community. In addition, the cross-denominational makeup of the Council was mainly successful early on "because many Reform and Conservative rabbis came from Orthodox backgrounds" (Golden, "From Cooperation to Confrontation," 142). This meant that, even as they identified with different denominations, they had a basic understanding and sympathy for the needs of their Orthodox counterparts. Taken together, the failure to embrace the full diversity of the American Jewish community by limiting membership to Conservative, Reform, and Orthodox rabbis; the organizational model; and the relative homogeneity of the members of the Council meant that, at least in its early decades of operation, its impact was rather limited.

The SCA faced a different challenge in the later decades of its existence. Unlike in former years, when there was greater homogeneity across the leaders of the three denominations, "[b]y the 1950s … it faced a new cadre of leaders who lived most, if not their entire, lives within the institutions of a particular movement and did not fraternize frequently, if at all, with members of other movements" (Golden, "From Cooperation to Confrontation," 142–143). As a result of the increasing alienation among rabbis from different denominations, "efforts to develop local branches of the Synagogue Council and to establish the kind of discourse necessary to carry out its work [were hampered]" (Golden, "From Cooperation to Confrontation," 143).

The challenges facing the SCA were compounded in the 1950s as a more ideologically conservative American Orthodoxy began to strengthen. In 1956, the SCA confronted a "ban on contacts between Orthodox rabbis and their Reform and Conservative counterparts" that was signed by ten prominent *haredi* Orthodox rabbis, including the influential leaders Moshe Feinstein and Aaron Kotler. The ban read in part:

> We have ... been asked if it is permissible to participate with and be a member of the Synagogue Council of America, which is also composed of Reform and Conservative organizations. We have ruled that it is forbidden by the law of our sacred Torah to participate with them either as an individual or as an organized communal body. (Sarna, "The Relationship of Orthodox Jews," 19)

The ban was just the latest challenge to the SCA that was, by the final decades of its existence, undermined from within and assailed from without. Even though the ultimate demise of the SCA in 1994 was the result of financial difficulties, "few, if any, in the American Jewish community were surprised" (Golden, "From Cooperation to Confrontation," 138).[25]

The examples of B'nai B'rith, the Jewish Welfare Board, Hillel, and the Synagogue Council of America illustrate the challenges that

---

25 According to Golden: "Upon hearing about the expiration of the SCA, one Orthodox leader recited 'Shehechiyanu' [a blessing of thanksgiving] for the end of an organization deemed illegitimate" (Golden, "From Cooperation to Confrontation," 138).

American Jewish organizations faced in responding to the increasing denominationalism of American Jewish life. B'nai B'rith attempted to sidestep denominational tensions altogether, while the JWB did arrive at a compromise, but only in a very limited context. Hillel and the SCA turned to pluralism as a way of confronting the increasingly splintered American Jewish community, with varying levels of success.

Irving Greenberg came of age in the late 1940s and early 1950s, just as denominational tensions were reaching their peak, exemplified by the Orthodox ban against the SCA. Although he would embrace the language of pluralism, his ideas and programs[26] ultimately went further than anything that had come before in their attempts to foster greater communal understanding and cooperation. Building on the respect for non-Orthodox Jews that he learned from his father, a deep sensitivity to ethics from his training in *Musar,* and the intellectual honesty of a trained historian, Greenberg embarked on a career that would offer a unique response to the changing realities of the American Jewish community. Just as Greenberg's own trajectory was not isolated from the changes taking place in the broader American Jewish context—in fact, it was informed and shaped by them—so, too, the changes felt by American Jews in the twentieth century were not disconnected from the changes taking place in the broader context of religion in America. Before turning to the development of Greenberg's theology of Hybrid Judaism, I want to turn our attention to the broader context of religion in American to provide another, wider, frame from which to understand the reality to which Greenberg was responding.

---

26 Greenberg's programmatic impact was most powerfully felt through the work that he undertook at CLAL: The Jewish Center for Learning and Leadership, an organization that he founded and led for more than two decades. The work of CLAL is not the focus of this study, and is certainly worthy of its own consideration.

# Chapter 2

# The Study and Reality of Religion in America

Even as twentieth-century American Judaism underwent significant changes, religion in America in general was itself subject to a major reappraisal. One illustrative way to describe the changing understanding and reality of religion in America is to look at the historiographical record. By examining the way that American religious history has been written over time, we can see how our understanding of religion in America has evolved and what that means for our changing understanding of identity.

It is widely acknowledged that the writing of American religious history proper began with Robert Baird's *Religion in America* (1844) and Philip Schaff's *America: A Sketch of the Political, Social, and Religious Character of the United States of North America* (1855). Baird (1798–1863), himself an Evangelical Protestant minister, described the history of American religion in theological more than historical terms. Dividing all American religions into two categories—"evangelical" and "non-evangelical"—he included groups such as Jews, Atheists, and Socialists in the latter category. As R. Laurence Moore has pointed out, Baird's theological outlook directly influenced the historical narrative that he portrayed, including his minimization of the growing role of Roman Catholics and Mormons in American religious life (R. Moore, *Religious Outsiders*, 5–9). Philip Schaff (1819–1893), a Swiss-born and German-trained historian of Christianity who arrived in the United States in the 1840s, took a similar approach. Described as "probably the most learned Protestant theologian and scholar who worked in the United States during the nineteenth century" (R. Moore, *Religious Outsiders*, 7), Schaff shared a religious and theological worldview in common with Baird. According to Moore, "As with Baird, Schaff's sense of what God intended guided his choices of what to emphasize about American religious life and what to play down" (R. Moore, *Religious Outsiders*, 8).

For more than a century after Baird's and Schaff's books were first published, historical treatments of American religion largely followed a similar approach. The story they told of religion in America failed to acknowledge the full extent of religious diversity that was actually present on the American religious landscape. The authors of the texts that followed in the footsteps of Baird and Schaff were primarily "church historians" engaged in the production of salvation histories.[1] They were often clergymen or professors at universities from the Northeast that were originally established as religious seminaries[2] and rarely ventured out of the close confines of New England Protestantism. The result was a predictable narrative of American religious history. As Catherine Albanese has written, "... when we look at America's ... religious history books ... we find that they generally tell one major story ... For if you tell the one story of America, perforce, it will center on the history-makers, the Anglo-Saxon and Protestant majority—and perhaps those most like them ... " (Albanese, *America*, xv). The result of telling "the one story" is that it "suppresses the distinctive identities of the many peoples who count themselves part of the American venture" (Albanese, *America*, xvi).

The historiographical limitations of such narratives, though oblivious to early scholars such as Baird and Schaff, have become more apparent to subsequent historians of American religious

---

1 Salvation histories are works by Christian historians that look for evidence of God's saving role in human history. For an excellent consideration of the development of church history in the American academy, see Jerald C. Brauer, ed., *Reinterpretations in American Church History* (Chicago: The University of Chicago Press, 1968).

2 This phenomenon was not limited to the nineteenth century, as Amanda Porterfield has noted: "Before 1975, many of the faculty teaching religious studies in colleges and universities received their advanced degrees from mainline Protestant divinity schools, and the curricula developed in those schools provided models for curricular programs in religious studies" (Cohen and Numbers, *Gods in America*, 23).

history. The earlier historiographical trend that emphasized Protestant hegemony and overlooked the fullness of religious diversity in America has become known as the *consensus narrative* of American religious history (Albanese, "American Religious History," 5–6). Thomas Tweed has also described it as "the old 'grand narrative' of consensus and progress in American history, which was peopled by white males and set in public places." He added that "attempt[s] to tell 'the whole story' of U.S. religious history have focused disproportionately on male, northeastern, Anglo-Saxon, mainline Protestants[3] and their beliefs, institutions, and power" (Tweed, *Retelling U.S. Religious History*, 3). This approach to American religious history had an impact beyond just the realm of professional scholars. As Albanese reminded her readers, "when the common-school movement spread across the United States … the models came from New England" (Albanese, *America*, 14), thus privileging a single dominant narrative of American religious history throughout the education system. In addition, the white male dominance in the field was also reflective of the balance of power between whites and non-whites and males and females in society in general. Taken together, these factors outline the sources of the emphasis towards the white, male, northeastern, and mainline Protestant version of American religious history. Because of the hegemony of the consensus narrative, it was not until the second half of the twentieth century, when traditional power structures would be disrupted, that a number of key developments would significantly shift the historiographical tide.

The pivot point upon which the consensus narrative turned toward a more inclusive and pluralistic approach to writing American religious history came with the 1972 publication of Sydney Ahlstrom's *A Religious History of the American People*. Ahlstrom's work represented both the culmination of the consensus narrative and the beginning

---

3  Mainline Protestant churches include (among others) the United Methodist Church, the Presbyterian Church, and the Episcopal Church. Until the middle of the twentieth century, these denominations represented a majority of Christians in the United States. The growth of the more conservative, Evangelical wing of the Protestant Church played a significant role in the decline of mainline Protestant churches.

of a new approach to telling the story of religion in America. Making this transition explicit in the final chapter of his book, Ahlstrom wrote that American religious history was "A Great Puritan Epoch" which "can be seen as beginning in 1558 with the death of Mary Tudor, the last Monarch to rule over an officially Roman Catholic England, and as ending in 1960 with the election of John Fitzgerald Kennedy, the first Roman Catholic president of the United States" (Ahlstrom, *A Religious History*, 1079). Critics have suggested that Ahlstrom's description was still too reminiscent of Baird's and other expressions of the consensus narrative, especially due to its lamenting tone for the passing of the Puritan Epoch.[4] Nevertheless, Ahlstrom concluded his massive book[5] with a section entitled "Toward Post-Puritan America," in which he addressed topics such as "Twentieth-Century Judaism," "Roman Catholicism in the Twentieth Century," "Piety for the Age of Aquarius: Theosophy, Occultism, and Non-Western Religion," and "Black Religion in the Twentieth Century." In these chapters, readers encountered the first inklings of a serious historical treatment of religious diversity in America. As Tweed has correctly observed, "Ahlstrom, and most authors who have followed him, have scripted scenes for the 'others' to play" (Tweed, *Retelling U.S. Religious History*, 13).

In the more than 40 years since the publication of Ahlstrom's magnum opus, an increasing number of books have expanded the telling of American religious history beyond "church history," with its theological, creedal, and confessional limitations, to allow for a more inclusive American religious history.[6] They have given non-Evangelicals, non-Protestants, women, non-whites, southerners,

---

4  Sidney Mead's "By Puritans Possessed" is still the strongest critique of Ahlstrom's work. Mead took Ahlstrom to task for lamenting the "sad post-Protestant because post-Puritan world." See Sidney Mead, "By Puritans Possessed." *Worldview* (1973): 49–52.

5  Part IX runs just over 100 pages in a book that totals just fewer than 1,100 pages in total, not including the bibliography and index.

6  The most prominent among them are Catherine Albanese's textbook, *America: Religions and Religion* (1981), R. Laurence Moore's *Religious Outsiders and the Making of Americans* (1986), Thomas Tweed's *Retelling U.S. Religious History* (1997), Jonathan Sarna's edited collection *Minority Faiths and American Protestant Mainstream* (1998),

southwesterners, and westerners more central roles to play in the narrative. As David Hackett wrote in the introduction to the first edition of his reader, *Religion and American Culture* (1995), "Today the study of American religion continues to move away from an older, European American, male, middle-class, northeastern, Protestant narrative concerned primarily with churches and theology and toward a multicultural tale of Native Americans, African Americans, Catholics, Jews, and other groups" (Hackett, *Religion and American Culture*, xi). The result has been what could be described as a more pluralistic assessment of the American religious landscape.

Although Ahlstrom's great work was not published until 1972, the origins of this historiographical shift can be located as far back as the first third of the twentieth century. Scholars at the University of Chicago played a critical role in the development of two influential schools of thought: the Chicago School of Sociology and the Chicago School of American Religious History. Scholars at the Chicago School of Sociology, such as Robert E. Park (1864–1944) and Louis Wirth (1897–1952), began to pay closer attention to the study of urban areas and social relations between different groups. This new approach to sociology was an early precursor to the "social history" movement that became popular in the latter part of the twentieth century in both history and religious studies departments. One result of this development was greater attention devoted to the lives of Americans *as they were actually lived*, as opposed to the way they were imagined by earlier scholars who had rarely come into direct contact with diversity or, worse still, simply disregarded it in their narratives of American religious history. Social history, also often referred to as the study of "lived religion," may best be described as "explorations of Americans' everyday experiences of religion" (Schultz and Harvey, "Everywhere and Nowhere," 142–143).

The second school that played a critical role in the development of American religious historiography was that of American Religious History. Scholars from the University of Chicago led the way in

and William R. Hutchison's *Religious Pluralism in America: The Contentious History of a Founding Ideal* (2003).

developing the field and generating new ways of thinking about American religious history that were independent of the theological presuppositions that characterized the work of Baird, Schaff, and the subsequent generations of scholars of American religious history that followed in their wake. In doing so, these new scholars were able to advance the field beyond just the writing of church histories. R. Laurence Moore has documented this shift and highlighted the central role that William Warren Sweet (1881–1958) played in this development. Moore has stated that Sweet "deserves the credit for establishing American religious history as an area of separate academic inquiry" (R. Moore, *Religious Outsiders*, 14). As a result of Sweet's contributions, "Chicago became the center of the discipline" (Brauer, *Reinterpretation in American Church History*, viii). Sweet was insistent that religious studies could be "an area of research that a secular-minded historian might tackle as appropriately as a minister or divinity school instructor" (R. Moore, *Religious Outsiders*, 14). If he was correct, religious history could be written by scholars without a theological stake in the game. Contrasted with Baird's and Schaff's religiously inspired version of events, this development represented an important shift in the way that American religious history would be written in the twentieth century and beyond.[7]

These developments were complemented by the postmodernist critique that first began to appear in the 1950s and 1960s. Postmodernism impacted a wide variety of disciplines, including the way that history in general, and religious history in particular, would be written. Postmodern thinkers generated a set of critical tools that were used to deconstruct grand narratives that pursued objectivity and attempted to tell "the whole story" from one particular vantage point.[8] Jean Lyotard has bluntly written that, "I define *postmodern* as

---

7 Although, as recently as 2005, Tomoko Masuzawa has opined that contemporary religious studies departments still have a "higher concentration of unreconstituted religious essentialists ... than anywhere else in the academy" (Masuzawa, *The Invention of World Religions*, 7).

8 The consensus narrative of American religious history is one such grand narrative.

incredulity toward metanarratives" (Rosman, *How Jewish is Jewish History?*, 16). For historians, this has meant that

> Gender, race, class, ethnicity, geographical location, cultural heritage, sociology, anthropology, demography, psychology, economics, and so on—all offer a unique perspective from which to produce a different, and valid, portrayal-cum-interpretation of past events. There is no 'God's-eye-view' of history that humans can produce. There are histories, not one unitary history. (Rosman, *How Jewish is Jewish History?*, 10)

The impact of the postmodern critique has been far reaching; however, for our purposes, it will suffice to recognize that it has provided a basis for more complex historical narratives that tell multiple stories from multiple perspectives. Moreover, it has not only called for greater inclusivity in the narration of American religious history, but also for the production of new narratives.

Despite the influence of postmodernism, there are still scholars who have continued to appeal to aspects of the consensus model. In 2001, the historian George Marsden complained that the increasing fragmentation of the field of American religious history has served to undermine "attempts to provide a coherent narrative in American religious history" (Marsden, *Religion and American Culture*, 15) and that "[t]he story of American religion, if it is to hang together as a narrative, must focus on the role played by certain groups of mainstream Protestants who were for a long time the insiders with disproportional influence in American culture" (Tweed, *Retelling U.S. Religious History*, 13). In his 2003 book, *Religious Pluralism in America*, William Hutchison has also suggested that, while some have asked that "we try to get along without broad interpretations of any kind for American religious history ... that cure would be worse than the disease." Accordingly, Hutchison has claimed that "we need organizing propositions, however tentative, if we are to get around intellectually in a messy world of particulars" (Hutchison, *Religious Pluralism*, 2).

Despite these protests, the consensus narrative is primarily employed by scholars today to describe the contours of American religious *historiography* rather than as a tool with which to actually write American religious *history*.

The historiographical shift from the consensus model toward a greater acknowledgment of diversity has been influenced by other factors on the American religious landscape. One such factor is the impact of immigration. By the 1880s, Asian immigrants to the United States already numbered more than 100,000 and brought with them "such 'foreign' religions as Confucianism and Buddhism" (Gaustad and Schmidt, *The Religious History of America*, 219). A massive wave of European immigrants arrived on American shores in the decades between 1880 and 1920 that shifted the U.S. population in an unprecedented manner and helped to recontour the American religious landscape. These new European immigrants included a population increase of American Jews by approximately 3 million and a Catholic population that grew at three times the rate of growth of the general population. In addition, there was also growth in the number of new Christian denominations during this time, including African-American Protestant denominations (Hutchison, *Religious Pluralism*, 114). These changes would not only impact the diversity of American citizenry, but they would also influence who would actually be writing American religious history in subsequent decades. For example, Jacob Rader Marcus (1896–1995), the American-born son of an immigrant family, went on to become the founding figure of American Jewish studies and established the American Jewish Archives in Cincinnati, Ohio, in 1947. Just the example of Marcus alone speaks to the impact of immigration around the turn of the twentieth century on the subsequent writing of American religious history.

In 1921 and 1924, the U.S. Congress passed the Johnson Act and the Johnson-Reed Act, respectively, both of which served to severely limit the number of European immigrants that would be admitted into the country. It was not until the passing of the Immigration and Nationality Act of 1965 that immigration would again play as significant a role as it had in the decades immediately before and after the turn of the twentieth century. David MacHacek has suggested that the "new religious pluralism" of the 1960s resulted not only from "the presence of Buddhists, Hindus, Sikhs, Muslims, and others among the post-1965 immigrants" but also because

> the cultural environment into which the post-1965 immigrants [were] being received ha[d] changed significantly ... In brief, the post-1965 immigrants, unlike earlier immigrants, stepped into a society that was rejecting a culture of communitarian consensus in favor of a culture that placed a positive value on diversity and dissent—that is, a culture of pluralism. (MacHacek, "The Problem of Pluralism," 146–148)

In effect, the "turbulent sixties" was a time when more than just the demographic facts on the ground were shifting; the attitudes of Americans across the country were shifting as well. With a much more diverse and contested religious landscape that included religious faiths from all over the world as well as home-grown religions, all within a context in which diversity was becoming more accepted, a new historiographical paradigm emerged that began to foster new narratives of American religious history.

With greater recognition of American diversity came new research agendas in university history and religious studies departments. These shifts, combined with the new scholarly methodologies of social history and postmodernism, resulted in, among other things, a significant reappraisal of American religious history and the historiographical approaches to researching and writing it.

Ironically, even as a more pluralistic narrative of American religious history became more commonplace, it also became outdated. Scholars were more attentive to the complexities of their subjects' lives, and thus came to the realization that it was no longer adequate to cast religion in America simply in terms of multiplicity. In his contribution to the 1993 forum, "The Decade Ahead in Scholarship,"

Robert Orsi, one of the exemplars of the "lived religion" approach to the study of American religious history, wrote:

> Imagine a day in the life of a white, middle-class, middle-aged woman in the middle years of this century. (She was born in Appalachia but is living at the time we encounter her in Baltimore.) She consults her astrological chart in the morning … In the afternoon, she practices some form of self-help physical or psychological therapy (which may be rooted in a complex cosmology and anthropology quite at odds with the perspectives of her denomination). Then she visits her (Freudian, Rogerian, Jungian, Sullivanian, or existentialist) analyst in the early evening, just before the meeting of her reading group at church, which tonight is taking up the issue, "The Edges of Life: Can They be Determined? (or perhaps exploring "Religions of the East," or, earlier in the century, "What is Christian Science All About?" or, even more disorienting, Emerson's essay on nature). (Orsi, "The Decade Ahead," 5–6)

In this excerpt, the complexity of the woman's religious life is immediately recognizable (even if she herself is unaware of it). Orsi's rendition of "a day in the life" is a far cry from the grand narratives of Robert Baird, but it also captures much more than just religious pluralism. This rendition of religion in America alerts us to the nature of religious diversity that is increasingly found in America today. Orsi's "white, middle-class, middle-aged woman" does not inhabit a singular religious world; rather, she has a complex religious life that intersects with multiple religious traditions. The increasing complexity of religious life in America contributes to the realization that pluralism—that is, simple diversity—is no longer adequate for describing, understanding, and interpreting religious lives and identities in America.

Courtney Bender and Pamela Klassen have identified other shortcomings of pluralism in their important book, *After Pluralism:*

*Reimagining Religious Engagement* (2010). Writing about pluralism from the perspective of religious group identity, they have observed that it fails to "adequately acknowledge the great diversity (and sometimes conflict) within particular religious traditions ..." (Bender and Klassen, *After Pluralism*, 12). Taking their critique one step further, Janet Jakobsen has suggested that

> the model of pluralism can fail to recognize both diversity within religious traditions and forms of religious difference that do not fit this model of organization, for example, those that are not organized around authorities who can act as spokespersons, that are not institutionalized in recognizable (and hierarchical) structures, and that are delineated by practice or land rather than by beliefs about which one might speak. (Jakobsen, "Ethics After Pluralism," 32)

The suggestion here is that pluralism not only fails to acknowledge diversity within religious communities, but that it also excludes certain individuals and groups that do not conform to normative expectations for what constitutes a religion or a religious community. Furthermore, Bender and Klassen have written that "the doctrines and programs of pluralism that dominate the contemporary academic and public conversations do not constitute a theory of understanding religious interactions as they take place in the world" (Bender and Klassen, *After Pluralism*, 12). The result is a pluralism discourse that projects and upholds a false image of the nature of religious diversity in American society.

By using this historiographical lens, it is clear that our understanding of the reality of religious life in America has changed dramatically since the days of Baird and Schaff. It is also clear that the increasing complexity of contemporary American Moment Judaisms fits into a broader trend affecting religious life in America more generally. Even as mid-twentieth century American Judaism was settling into a more ideological denominationalism, the changes taking place on the broader American religious landscape were undermining that trend. The historiographical lens also draws our attention to the centrally important topic of pluralism. As I will show in the next chapter, pluralism is a theory of individual and group identity that is based on the notion of firm boundaries both between and within groups. As such, it fails to acknowledge the full extent of religious diversity in the United States, or the manner in which diverse groups within and across religions interact and overlap. Before we can turn to Greenberg's theology of Hybrid Judaism in earnest, we need to understand the meaning of pluralism more fully and appreciate its shortcomings as a sociological theory of individual and group identity. It is to that topic that we now turn.

# Chapter 3

# The Arc, Part 1: From Melting Pot to Triple Melting Pot

We now shift our focus from religion in America to sociological theories of identity. The twentieth-century arc of sociological theories of individual identity and group life in America is our final stop before we turn to Greenberg's theology of Hybrid Judaism. In similar fashion to the way the historiographical lens helped demonstrate the changing understanding and reality of religion in America, the sociological lens will provide a framework with which to highlight the changing understanding and reality of individual identity and group life in America. Beginning with the melting pot and concluding with postethnicity, the century-long arc will center on pluralism and bring its shortcomings into clear relief.

The most familiar sociological theory of American group life is that of the melting pot. Notions of America as a melting pot date back to Hector St. John de Crèvecoeur's *Letters from an American Farmer* (1782), in which he observed that "Here individuals of all nations are melted into a new race of men" (Katkin, Landsman, and Tyree, *Beyond Pluralism*, 107). In the middle of the nineteenth century, Ralph Waldo Emerson compared contemporary America to the "smelting pot of the Dark Ages," and Herman Melville imagined American blood as "the flood of the Amazon ... a thousand noble currents all pouring into one" (Hutchison, *Religious Pluralism*, 190). However, it was not until Israel Zangwill's play, *The Melting Pot*, was staged in 1908 and subsequently published in 1909 that both the phrase and the concept began to hold wide currency in American society.

Zangwill (1864–1926), a British Jew who came to be known as the Jewish Dickens, was a prolific author and playwright, public intellectual, and influential political figure, especially with regard to the nascent question of Jewish statehood.[1] Zangwill's influential play, *The Melting Pot: A Drama in Four Acts* (1909), tells the improbable story of David Quixano and Vera Revendal, both immigrants to the United States from Russia. David and Vera fall in love and become betrothed to each other, despite the fact that David is a Jew and Vera a Christian. To further complicate matters, it is revealed during the third act that Vera's father, Baron Revendal, led the Russian pogrom that resulted in the murder of David's family and countless other Jews. Despite it all, the play closes with David embracing Vera and offering a final thought as they look out on a beautiful sunset:

> It is the fires of God round His Crucible. There she lies, the great Melting Pot—listen! Can't you hear the roaring and the bubbling? There gapes her mouth—the harbor where a thousand mammoth feeders come from the ends of the world to pour in their human freight. Ah, what a stirring and a seething! Celt and Latin, Slav and Teuton, Greek and Syrian, black and yellow. (Zangwill, *The Melting Pot*)

Vera adds: "Jew and Gentile." David continues:

> Yes, East and West, and North and South, the palm and the pine, the pole and the equator, the crescent and the cross—how the great Alchemist melts and fuses them with his purging flame! Here shall they all unite to build the Republic of Man and the Kingdom of God. Ah, Vera, what is the glory of Rome and Jerusalem where all nations and races come to

---

1 Ultimately, Zangwill became the leader of the Jewish Territorial Organisation (ITO), which was committed to finding a homeland for the Jewish people in a location other than Palestine. For a useful biographical treatment, see Joseph Leftwich, *Israel Zangwill* (New York: Thomas Yoseloff, 1957).

worship and look back, compared with the glory of America, where all races and nations come to labour and look forward! (Zangwill, *The Melting Pot*)

In these excerpts, David describes America as a country in which all peoples come to be melted together into "God's Crucible." It is a place where all prior differences can be overcome to create a new "Republic of Man" in which the citizens themselves take on a new collective identity. They are no longer Jewish, Christian, Russian, or German, but rather American.

Zangwill's melting pot came under fire from Anglo-conformists and Nativists[2] who were ill at ease with the idea that their conception of what it meant to be American might be diluted by the melting of immigrants into the cauldron of America. Others who read Zangwill's play balked at the idea that immigrants to America should abandon their ethnic, cultural, and religious heritage, or that they would be perfected through assimilation with other groups. Reading the play more than a century later, it is also clear that references to the "Republic of Man and the Kingdom of God" expressed a conception of the melting pot that would have sounded more familiar to Europeans—that is, Christians and Jews—than it would have to non-Europeans and those professing non-Biblical faiths. To be sure, even Jewish ears would find Zangwill's formulations a little too Christian for their

---

2 Anglo-conformists "demanded the complete renunciation of the immigrant's ancestral culture in favor of the behavior and values of the Anglo-Saxon group" (Gordon, *Assimilation in American Life*, 85). As for Nativists:

> Previously vague and romantic notions of Anglo-Saxon peoplehood were combined with general ethnocentrism, rudimentary wisps of genetics, selected tidbits of evolutionary theory, and naïve assumptions from an early and crude imported anthropology ... to produce the doctrine that the English, Germans, and others of the 'old immigrants' constituted a superior race of tall, blond, blue-eyed, 'Nordics' or 'Aryans,' whereas the peoples of Eastern and Southern Europe made up the darker Alpines or Mediterraneans—both inferior breeds whose presence in America threatened, either by intermixture or supplementation, the traditional American stock and culture. (Gordon, *Assimilation in American Life*, 97)

tastes. Certainly, the marriage of the play's central protagonists—a Jew and a Christian—invited the ire of many Jewish commentators.[3]

Nevertheless, the 1908 opening night of *The Melting Pot* was attended by President Theodore Roosevelt who, it is reported, "leaned over his box and shouted to Mr. Zangwill, 'It's a great play'" (Leftwich, *Israel Zangwill*, 252). The endorsement from Roosevelt, as well as a run of 136 performances, helped solidify the idea of the melting pot in the imagination of the American public. As David Biale has observed, "the play became a pivotal moment in the American debate about the mass immigration of the early part of the century. Zangwill did not invent the term 'melting pot,' but he was instrumental in popularizing its use in American political discourse ... " (Biale, "The Melting Pot and Beyond," 19). So much so that it "has continued to reverberate in a variety of incarnations and reincarnations" (Biale, "The Melting Pot and Beyond," 19). Zangwill's melting pot represented the beginning point of the century-long arc of attempts at describing group life in America. The next point along that arc came from an outspoken critic of Zangwill and the melting pot.

Horace Meyer Kallen (1882–1974) was born into a rabbinic family in Germany and immigrated with his parents to the United States in 1887. Settling in Boston, Kallen attended Harvard College, earning his bachelor's degree and a doctorate in philosophy. Following a seven-year teaching post at the University of Wisconsin-Madison, Kallen helped to establish the New School for Social Research in New York City and joined its faculty in 1919, where he taught until a year before his death. Despite thoroughly rejecting his father's Orthodoxy, Kallen became an influential leader in the American Jewish community. He played a significant role in the establishment of the Menorah Society at Harvard College and supported the growth

---

3 For example, "Rabbi Answers Zangwill." November 16, 1908. *The New York Times.* For a detailed analysis of the play, see Werner Sollors, *Beyond Ethnicity: Consent and Descent in American Culture* (New York: Oxford University Press, 1986): 66–101.

of the Intercollegiate Menorah Association on other college campuses.[4] These organizations promoted "Jewish culture as a means to foster pride" and their founders, Kallen among them, "hoped that their study as well as their fellowship would combat the 'indifference' and 'shameful ignorance of things Jewish'" (Greene, *The Jewish Origins*, 28–29). In addition, Kallen was a staunch supporter of Zionism, serving as a founding delegate to the American Jewish Congress (Pianko, *"The True Liberalism of Zionism"*, 302), and was often engaged in the cause for Jewish education, serving as vice-president of the American Association of Jewish Education, among other roles (Kronish, "John Dewey," 142).

Horace Kallen's most significant contribution, however, was his formulation of the concept of cultural pluralism as a response to Zangwill's melting pot idea and to notions of Anglo-conformity and nativism. Although he did not coin the term "cultural pluralism" until 1924,[5] he began writing about group identity in America as early as 1906.[6] It was in the pages of *The Nation*, a weekly publication devoted to politics and culture, that Kallen published what would become one of his most well-known essays, entitled "Democracy versus the Melting Pot: A Study of American Nationality" (1915). Responding to his Wisconsin-Madison colleague and Nativist thinker, Edward Alsworth Ross (1866–1951), Kallen argued that, rather than posing a threat to the United States, immigrants, and the cultural diversity they brought with them, supported the democratic ideals that defined America.

Turning to Zangwill's melting pot, Kallen claimed that, rather than melting into each other, immigrants could become American

---

4 For an excellent intellectual biography of Kallen, cultural pluralism, and the Menorah Association, see Daniel Greene, *The Jewish Origins of Cultural Pluralism: The Menorah Association and American Diversity.* (Bloomington: Indiana University Press, 2011).

5 The term "cultural pluralism" was first used by Kallen in his essay, "Culture and the Ku Klux Klan." See Horace Kallen, *Culture and Democracy in the United States* (New Brunswick: Transaction Publishers, 1998 (1924)).

6 See Horace Kallen, "The Ethics of Zionism." *Maccabean* 11, no. 2 (1906): 61–71.

precisely as a result of holding on to their cultural particularity. In Kallen's words:

> ... the outlines of a possible great and truly democratic commonwealth become discernible. Its form is that of a Federal republic; its substance a democracy of nationalities, cooperating voluntarily and autonomously through common institutions in the enterprise of self-realization through the perfection of men according to their kind. The common language of the commonwealth, the language of its great tradition, would be English, but each nationality would have for its emotional and involuntary life its own particular dialect or speech, its own individual and inevitable esthetic and intellectual forms ... Thus "American civilization" may come to mean the perfection of the cooperative harmonies of "European Civilization" ... (Kallen, *Culture and Democracy*, 116)

Kallen's vision was clear: America should not be a melting pot, nor should it respond to its newest immigrants in Anglo-conformist or nativist terms, because their diverse ethnic identities were "involuntary," and therefore inevitable.

Just a few months after Kallen's essay appeared in *The Nation*, he returned to the subject of cultural pluralism (although not yet by that name) in an essay published in *The Menorah Journal* entitled "Nationality and the Hyphenated American" (1915). In this essay, Kallen looked to Switzerland as a model for American democracy. Kallen observed that " ... the nationhood of Switzerland is the most integral and unified in Europe to-day, because Switzerland is as complete and thorough a democracy as exists in the civilized world, and the efficacious safeguard of nationhood is democracy not only of individuals but of nationalities" (Kallen, "Nationality and the Hyphenated American," 80). For Kallen, a country populated by a diverse citizenry could only be truly democratic if the multiplicity of nationalities present remained distinct and were protected. As such, Kallen believed that citizens of the United States should be empowered to carry dual identities. Kallen called this the "hyphenated American" and suggested that for "American nationhood ... its democracy is its strength, and its democracy is 'hyphenation'" (Kallen, "Nationality and the Hyphenated American," 82).[7] A year after the publication of Kallen's two essays, the American philosopher and educational reformer, John Dewey, echoed Kallen's ideas and implored his audience at the National Educational Association that "the genuine American, the typical American, is himself a hyphenated character" (Gordon, *Assimilation in American Life,* 139). Put differently, Kallen (and Dewey) did not simply believe that America had a responsibility to protect the diverse peoples within its borders, but rather that the different peoples themselves had a responsibility to hold on to their ethnic and cultural identities to protect American democracy.

Kallen's vision of Cultural Pluralism was far reaching in its acceptance and encouragement of ethnic diversity and placed great importance on the retention of group boundaries. In the closing paragraph of "Democracy versus the Melting Pot," Kallen used a powerful simile to make his point:

> As in an orchestra, every type of instrument has its specific timbre and tonality, founded in its substance and form; as every type has its appropriate theme and melody in the whole symphony, so in society each ethnic group is the natural instrument, its spirit and culture are its theme and melody, and the harmony and dissonances and discords of

---

7 W. E. B. Du Bois's notion of "double consciousness," while not identical, had much in common with Kallen's notions of cultural pluralism and hyphenation. As Daniel Greene has noted, "In 1897, just a decade before Kallen began to publish on pluralism, Du Bois famously asked, 'What, after all, am I? Am I an American or am I a Negro? Can I be both? Or is it my duty to cease to be a Negro as soon as possible and be an American?'" (Greene, *The Jewish Origins,* 8). As Greene has also pointed out, the question of race—specifically, the situation of African-Americans—was a significant "blind spot" for Kallen (Greene, *The Jewish Origins,* 7–8).

them all make the symphony of civilization. (Kallen, *Culture and Democracy*, 116–117)

In his use of the image of the orchestra, Kallen proposed that the different ethnic groups in a diverse society should have fixed and distinct identities. Werner Sollors, in his "Critique of Pure Pluralism," has explained Kallen's orchestral metaphor in this way:

> ... the stable quality of each instrument must be preserved. Kallen's definition of cultural pluralism rests on quasi-eternal, static units, on the "distinctive individuality of each *natio* [sic]" ... on "ancestry," "homogeneity of heritage, mentality and interest," and mankind's "psycho-physical inheritance." (Sollors, "A Critique of Pure Pluralism," 260)

David Hollinger has also written that, in employing the metaphor of the orchestra, Kallen "emphasized the integrity and autonomy of each descent-defined group" (Hollinger, *Postethnic America*, 92). Put simply, ethnic identity was, for Kallen, fixed. Kallen memorably underlined this point at the end of "Democracy versus the Melting Pot" when he wrote: "Men may change their clothes, their politics, their wives, their religions, their philosophies, to a greater or lesser extent: they cannot change their grandfathers. Jews or Poles or Anglo-Saxons, in order to cease being Jews or Poles or Anglo-Saxons, would have to cease to be ... " (Kallen, *Culture and Democracy*, 114–115).[8] Kallen's point was two-fold: first, ethnic groups have hereditary identities that they cannot escape[9] and, second, that the identities of each group, like the instruments in the orchestra, are, and should

---

8  It is noteworthy that Kallen, himself a secular Jew, considered Jewish identity an ethnic/cultural designation and not a religious one. See footnote 10.

9  Daniel Greene has given some attention to the fact that, although "By the mid-1920s, Kallen had set aside the notion of descent-based identity," critics "tended to remember him for what they interpreted as a theory of identity that essentialized descent" (Greene, *The Jewish Origins*, 89, 183). However, even if one removes the notion of descent-based identity, cultural pluralism stills calls for sharp boundaries between groups, regardless of how individuals come to be associated with them.

remain, distinct from one another. Writing as a Jewish, European-born immigrant who called for equal acceptance of Hebraism[10] in America, Kallen declared that the boundaries of cultural identity needed to be sharply drawn and strongly upheld if democracy was to be successful.

In his book, *American Pluralism: A Study of Minority Groups and Social Theory* (1973), sociologist William M. Newman used mathematical equations to represent different models of social interaction.[11] Kallen's theory—Newman called it "Classical Cultural Pluralism"—is represented thus: $A + B + C = A + B + C$. Represented in this way, each group (A, B, and C) maintains its own identity even as it lives alongside other groups (Newman, *American Pluralism*, 67). As David Hollinger has explained it, pluralism intends "to protect and perpetuate particular, existing cultures" (Hollinger, *Postethnic America*, 85).

The ideas in "Democracy versus the Melting Pot" and "Nationality and the Hyphenated America" were combined and given the name "Cultural Pluralism" by Kallen in his 1924 collection of essays, *Culture and Democracy in the United States*.[12] Although mostly a collection

---

10  Hebraism was "an identity grounded in scholarly study of Jewish history and culture" (Greene, *The Jewish Origins*, 16) and looked to the *Verein für Cultur und Wissenschaft der Juden* (Association for the Culture and Science of the Jews) for its inspiration. As such, Kallen was not sympathetic to religious expressions of Jewish group life. Daniel Greene has described it thus:

> Kallen advocated that [Hebraism] replace religion as the cornerstone of Jewish self-understanding ... As Kallen wrote to Judge Julian Mack in 1915, 'Religion is less than life, and as life becomes more secularized, the religion of the Jews becomes less and less the life of the Jews. I use the word Hebraism consequently to designate the whole of that life, of which Judaism is a part ... ' (Greene, *The Jewish Origins*, 33)

11  I first encountered Newman's work in Michael Kay, *The Paradox of Pluralism: Leadership and Community Building in Pluralistic Jewish High Schools*. PhD diss., New York University, 2009.

12  Although the term did not appear in print until 1924, Kallen had already been using it for a number of years. He recounted the origins of the idea thus:

> It was in 1905 that I began to formulate the notion of cultural pluralism and I had to do that in connection with my teaching. I was assisting both Mr. [William] James and Mr. [George] Santayana at the time and I had a Negro student named Alain Locke, a very remarkable young man—very sensitive, very easily hurt—who insisted that he was a human being and that his color ought not to make any difference. And, of course, it was a mistaken insistence. It *had* to make a difference and it *had* to be accepted

of previously published essays, Kallen added a "Postscript—To Be Read First" to the volume, entitled "Culture and the Ku Klux Klan." At the essay's conclusion, Kallen declared that, "Cultural Pluralism is possible only in a democratic society whose institutions encourage individuality in groups, in persons, in temperaments … the alternative before Americans is Kultur Klux Klan or Cultural Pluralism" (Kallen, *Culture and Democracy*, 35). For Horace Kallen, Cultural Pluralism meant more than just an "acceptance and encouragement of diversity," as William R. Hutchison has defined it. Rather, he intended to make a claim about the nature of ethnic group identity and the very nature of democracy. According to Kallen, democracy could not exist without cultural pluralism and cultural pluralism was predicated on the maintenance of distinct group identities.

The differences between Kallen and Zangwill are stark. Where Zangwill imagined an America in which all differences were "melted away" to create a new breed of American for whom religion, culture, or ethnic identity was no longer a barrier to assimilation, Kallen saw it as a place where cultural and ethnic differences could, and should, be retained and where immigrant groups would maintain clear boundaries between themselves and other groups. As Daniel Greene has noted,

> Kallen's pluralist vision … relied on imagining the nation as a conglomerate of co-existing groups. He said little about cooperation and rejected the premise that cultures somehow would meld together to form a new homogenized American culture … The duty of each ethnic group within a nation was therefore to ensure political harmony but at the same

---

and respected and enjoyed for what it was. Two years later when I went to Oxford on a fellowship he was there as a Rhodes scholar, and we had a race problem because the Rhodes scholars from the South were bastards. So they had a Thanksgiving dinner which I refused to attend because they refused to have Locke. And he said, 'I am a human being,' just as I had said it earlier. What difference does the difference make. We are all alike Americans. And we had to argue out the question of how the differences made differences, and in arguing out those questions the formulae, then the phrases, developed—'cultural pluralism,' 'the right to be different.' (Sollors, "A Critique of Pure Pluralism," 269)

time to resist cultural or biological uniformity. (Greene, *The Jewish Origins*, 73)

In contrast to the melting pot, hyphenation and the model of the Swiss Cantons that Kallen found so appealing informed a conception of cultural pluralism that pointed to harmonious coexistence along with a commitment to retaining clear group boundaries.

The question of precisely how, according to Kallen, the different groups in American society would be able to coexist while still retaining their distinct identities was raised by the sociologist Milton Gordon in his important book, *Assimilation in American Life: The Role of Race, Religion, and National Origins* (1964). Gordon wrote that, "If one inquires ... as to the specific nature of the communication and interaction which is to exist between the various ethnic communities and between individuals who compose them in the 'ideal' cultural pluralistic societies, the answer does not emerge clearly from Kallen's descriptions" (Gordon, *Assimilation in American Life*, 148). As a result, Gordon concluded that

> Kallen's body of work on the cultural pluralism idea, remarkable and germinal as it is, tends to be embodied in a general framework of rhetoric and philosophical analysis which has not pushed to the fore that kind of rigorous sociological inquiry which the crucial importance of the idea ultimately demands. (Gordon, *Assimilation in American Life*, 149)

As Gordon pointed out, there is an inherent tension in Kallen's formulation of cultural pluralism: "On the one hand, he is opposed to 'ghetto' existence and group isolation and favors creative interaction. On the other hand, he is against the dissolution of the communities" (Gordon, *Assimilation in American Life*, 148). As a result, Kallen's cultural pluralism failed to account for what might happen, in Gordon's words, "when peoples meet" (Gordon, *Assimilation in American Life*, 60).[13]

---

13  Gordon's source for this phrase is from Alain Locke and Bernhard J. Stern, eds. *When Peoples Meet: A Study in Race and Culture Contacts* (New York: Hinds, Hayden & Eldridge, 1946).

Gordon's work surveyed a wide range of assimilatory trends in society that resulted from "peoples meeting." Accordingly, he distinguished between *primary relationships* and *secondary relationships*. Primary relationships, as defined by Gordon, are "personal, intimate, emotionally affective, and ... bring into play the whole personality," whereas secondary relationships are "impersonal, formal, and segmentalized, and tend not to come very close to the core of personality" (Gordon, *Assimilation in American Life*, 32). An appreciation of the impact of social contact on the level of Gordon's primary relationships—what I refer to as encounters—is critically important if we are to understand what happens "when peoples meet." For Kallen's cultural pluralism to manifest, it "demands keeping primary group relations across ethnic lines sufficiently minimal to prevent a significant amount of intermarriage, while cooperating with other groups and individuals in the secondary relations areas of political action, economic life, and civic responsibility" (Gordon, *Assimilation in American Life*, 158). Put simply, Kallen failed to account for the importance, and increasing likelihood, of encounters across group lines. Of course, in the half century since Gordon published his book, let alone the century since Kallen's first explorations into cultural pluralism, the American social landscape has changed a great deal and primary relationships that cross group lines have become increasingly common. Kallen's failure to anticipate the increasing likelihood and implications of such encounters represents the central weakness of his theory of cultural pluralism.[14] America is not Kallen's imagined orchestra with neatly divided and organized groups living alongside one another. Moreover, when individuals and groups have no choice but to encounter one another as they so often do in the American open society, something undoubtedly happens.

The initial impact of Kallen's contribution to the century-long arc of sociological theories of group life in America was not

---

14  This is especially surprising due to the fact that Kallen entered into the most significant of primary relationships—marriage—with a non-Jewish woman.

comparable to Zangwill's idea of the melting pot. As one observer has put it, "The idea never gained as much traction in American cultural life as the melting pot did" (Greene, *The Jewish Origins*, 181–182). It is only from the vantage point of the late twentieth- and early twenty-first centuries that Kallen's influence looms so large. In fact, in the early part of the twentieth century, when Kallen published his most important essays on the subject of cultural pluralism, the idea did not make much of an impact at all. Nevertheless, although the language of cultural pluralism did not become widespread for many decades,[15] the concept did begin to have greater currency in the second half of the twentieth century, and the term "pluralism" was increasingly employed in scholarly literature and in general American discourse.[16]

From the vantage point of the twenty-first century, it is clear that Horace Kallen's theory of cultural pluralism represented a conceptual bridge from the Anglo-conformism, nativism, and melting pot-ism of the early twentieth century to notions of multiculturalism in the 1960s and 1970s. Even though Kallen and his theory of cultural pluralism were often taken to task by late twentieth-century multiculturalists because of the "biological determinism suggested by his 1915 claim that one could not change one's grandfather,"[17] (Greene, *The Jewish Origins*, 183) he was seen by others as a positive force whose "pluralist ambition was no small thing in its time" (Greene, *The Jewish Origins*, 184). Ultimately, and despite its theoretical and practical shortcomings, cultural pluralism has had an abiding influence on American self-understanding. By the middle of the twentieth

---

15  In an interview from 1972, Kallen pointed out that "cultural pluralism's time had finally come, adding that 'it's taken just about fifty years.'" Cited in Daniel Marom, "Who's Afraid of Horace Kallen? Cultural Pluralism and Jewish Education." *Studies in Jewish Education*. 13 (2009): 283–337.

16  A recent search on Hollis, the Harvard library online search engine, showed that the term "pluralism" does not begin to occur in double digits until the 1950s and 1960s, and only in the 1970s and 1980s does the term start to appear in the hundreds.

17  As noted earlier, Daniel Greene has convincingly shown that Kallen set aside these notions as early as the mid-1920s, but his critics "ignored this correction" (Greene, *The Jewish Origins*, 183).

century, it would be adapted by Will Herberg to address questions of religious, rather than ethnic, identity in America.

Despite his claims to birth in the United States, Will Herberg (1901–1977) was actually born in Russia and immigrated with his parents in 1904. He held a tenured position in Judaic Studies and Social Philosophy at Drew University, even though his academic pedigree was also the stuff of fiction—he had never actually earned the college degree and doctorate to which he made claim. Not unfamiliar with reinvention, Herberg was an avowed communist in his early life but rejected that ideology and embraced traditional Judaism, publishing the widely read treatise, *Judaism and the Modern Man* (1951). Despite his lack of formal training as a sociologist, his most significant contribution was his 1955 book, *Protestant-Catholic-Jew: An Essay in American Religious Sociology.* Martin Marty has described the book as "[t]he most honored discussion of American religion in mid-twentieth century times" (Herberg, *Protestant-Catholic-Jew,* vii). The book has seen multiple editions and is still a staple in contemporary college courses addressing religious life in America in the middle part of the twentieth century. It also represents the next point along the twentieth century arc of sociological theories of group life in America.

Although Herberg's conclusions and predictions have been described as failing "to anticipate almost every important turn in subsequent American life" (Herberg, *Protestant-Catholic-Jew,* x), the impact of his work on the American psyche around the time of its publication was significant. Herberg adapted Kallen's notion of cultural pluralism by turning his attention away from European ethnic groups and focusing instead on religious groups in America. As "an interpretation of the religious situation" in America, Herberg chose as his subject what he called the paradox of "pervasive secularism amid mounting religiosity" (Herberg, *Protestant-Catholic-Jew,* 2). His explanation of this apparent contradiction was that, as one scholar has put it, "American religion was shallow and meretricious ... To put it into modern parlance, American religion was a 'feel-good' religion" (Shapiro,

"Will Herberg's Protestant-Catholic-Jew," 262). The result was that a significant percentage of the American public professed religious beliefs while the rate of active participation in religious life was very low. More important than Herberg's ill regard for the quality of American religiosity was his estimation of the important role religious identity played in American life.[18]

In what might be described as a combination of Zangwill's Melting Pot and Kallen's Cultural Pluralism, Herberg suggested that American group life had, by the middle of the twentieth century, turned from division along ethnic lines to alignment along religious ones. In his words,

> Self-identification in ethnic terms, while it was a product of the American environment, was also a sign of incomplete integration into American life ... to the American mind an ethnic group that becomes permanent and self-perpetuating and resists cultural assimilation—in other words, what the European would call a 'national-cultural' minority—would appear as an alien 'race' ... (Herberg, *Protestant-Catholic-Jew*, 37–38)

However, rather than dissolving into an entirely new and homogeneous "American Republic of Man," as Zangwill's Quixano declared in 1909, Herberg's view was that "while America knows no national or cultural minorities except as temporary, transitional phenomena, it does know a free variety and plurality of religions ... " (Herberg, *Protestant-Catholic-Jew*, 38). In effect, Herberg affirmed Zangwill's notion that competing ethnicities were, or should be, melting together in the American cauldron even as he held on to a Kallenesque sense of group boundaries, although now with respect to religious life in America.

---

18 As Kevin Schultz has observed, only the latter of these two contributions "is much remembered" (Schultz, "Protestant-Catholic-Jew, Then and Now," http://www.first-things.com/article/2006/01/protestant-catholic-jewthen-and-now).

Building on the research of Ruby Jo Kennedy,[19] Herberg suggested that "America is indeed ... the land of the 'triple melting pot,'[20] for it is within these three religious communities that the process of ethnic and cultural integration so characteristic of American life takes place" (Herberg, *Protestant-Catholic-Jew*, 37). In terms that harken back to David Quixano, even as they invert his original intention, Herberg continued, "in each of these communities what emerges is a 'new man' cast and recast along the same 'American' ideal type" (Herberg, *Protestant-Catholic-Jew*, 37). For Herberg, Americans were defined by a shared American culture that included within it an attachment to one of three religious communities— Protestantism, Catholicism, or Judaism. Put simply, "[i]t is general conformity to this ideal type that makes us all Americans, just as it is the diversity of religious community that gives us our distinctive place in American society" (Herberg, *Protestant-Catholic-Jew*, 37).

Describing those individuals not identified with one of the three religions of the triple-melting pot, Herberg declared that "such people are few and far between in this country and are not even remotely significant in determining the American's understanding of himself ... Not to be a Catholic, a Protestant, or a Jew today is, for increasing numbers of American people, not to be anything, not to have a name ... " (Herberg, *Protestant-Catholic-Jew*, 39–40). And again, "Unless one is either a Protestant, or a Catholic, or a Jew, one is 'nothing'; to be a 'something,' to have a name, one must identify oneself, and be identified by others, as belonging to one or another of the three great religious communities in which the American

---

19  Ruby Jo Reeves Kennedy, "Single or Triple Melting Pot? Intermarriage Trends in New Haven, 1870–1940," *American Journal of Sociology* 49, no. 4 (1944). Cited in Herberg (*Protestant-Catholic-Jew*, 27–45).

20  The "melting pot" has taken on multiple meanings over the course of the last century. As Daniel Greene has pointed out, "The melting pot meant something significantly different by mid-century than it had in 1908. In fact, its meaning had changed almost entirely. By the 1960s the connotation of the melting pot actually resembled something close to what cultural pluralism had meant during the 1920s" (Greene, *The Jewish Origins*, 182).

people are divided" (Herberg, *Protestant-Catholic-Jew*, 40). Herberg could not have been more mistaken.

In the decades since the publication of *Protestant-Catholic-Jew*, Herberg has been much criticized for his (mis)characterization of what it meant to be an American. His overly homogeneous picture of American religious life missed the rise of Protestant Evangelicalism, which already counted close to 10 million adherents by the 1950s. He also ignored the increasing religious diversity in America that resulted from rising immigration from Asia. The fact that, like Kallen, Herberg paid scant attention to African-Americans also left him open to criticism.[21]

Despite the scholarly shortcomings of Herberg's book, it still served as a highly influential text, selling widely and receiving positive reviews in *The New York Times* (Schultz, "Catholic-Protestant-Jew, Then and Now"). It also reinforced a popular theme in 1950s America that viewed the United States through the lens of the culture war with the Soviet Union. Many Americans believed that what distinguished them from "godless communism" was America's commitment to religion. In a sense, Herberg's book served to underline and reinforce this point and echoed President-elect Dwight Eisenhower's 1952 comment that "our government makes no sense unless it is founded in a deeply felt religious faith—and I don't care what it is" (Hutchison, *Religious Pluralism*, 198).

It is also significant that Herberg's book "served as a kind of 'scientific' legitimation of the arrival of American Jews as partners on the national religious scene, bolstering Jewish self-respect and altering for the better the perceptions of American Jews held by their non-Jewish neighbors" (Shapiro, "Will Herberg's Protestant-Catholic-Jew," 271). A similar dynamic can be noted with regard to Catholics who, until the election of President Kennedy in 1960, also experienced a quasi-outsider status in America. The simple fact that a respected scholar had published a popular book about religious

---

21 For a laundry list of shortcomings of Herberg's observations, see Edward Shapiro, "Will Herberg's Protestant-Catholic-Jew: A Critique." Jack Kugelmass, ed. *Key Texts in American Jewish Culture*. (New Brunswick: Rutgers University Press, 2003): 258–274.

life in America with the words "Jew" and "Catholic" alongside "Protestant" meant a great deal to the growing sense of comfort felt by members of those religious communities.[22] Herberg believed that Judaism had a part to play alongside Protestantism and Catholicism as a religious tradition that supported deeply held American values.

It is worthwhile to recall that Herberg published *Protestant-Catholic-Jew* in 1955. At that time, American citizens were just beginning to confront many of the issues that would come to the fore in what Sydney Ahlstrom would retrospectively call "the turbulent sixties." In 1954, the Supreme Court would declare that segregation in the public schools was unconstitutional. In the same decade, the civil rights movement would gain steam with the Montgomery Bus Boycott of 1955, highlighted by the actions of Rosa Parks. The 1960s would bring a rising interest in the rights of Native Americans, highlighted by the occupation of Alcatraz by the activist group "Indians of All Tribes" at the end of that decade. In addition, the sexual revolution, the Black Power Movement, the growing public face of the Nation of Islam, an increasing interest in Eastern religions, and a general antiestablishment feeling resulting from the growing dissatisfaction with the Vietnam War would all contribute to new narratives about American group identity. Questions of culture, ethnicity, race, religion, and the role of women in society would all come to the fore during this time (it would take a little while longer for questions of sexual and gender identity to enter the national conversation) and challenge all previous theories of group life in the United States. As ethnic and cultural pride increased, suggestions that distinct communities would melt into each other became increasingly unpopular. At the same time, Herberg's suggestion that Americans had to choose from Protestantism, Catholicism, or Judaism seemed absurd. As soon as *Protestant-Catholic-Jew* hit the bookstores it had, in large part, become obsolete.

---

22 Nonetheless, the title of the book still suffered from the fact that the three faiths were not listed alphabetically, implicitly suggesting that a hierarchy was still in place, at least to some extent.

# Chapter 4

# The Arc, Part 2: From Multiculturalism to Postethnicity

Less than a decade after the publication of *Protestant-Catholic-Jew*, Nathan Glazer coauthored a book that would advance the thinking about individual and group identity one step further. Born in New York City in 1923, Glazer, like Horace Kallen and Will Herberg before him, was the child of immigrant parents. A Columbia-trained sociologist, Glazer went on to a long and illustrious career as a professor at the Harvard Graduate School of Education.[1] One of his most important contributions was the book that he coauthored with then-counselor to President Richard Nixon, Daniel Patrick Moynihan (1927–2003), *Beyond the Melting Pot: The Negroes, Puerto Ricans, Jews, Italians, and Irish of New York City* (1963/1970).

Glazer and Moynihan offered a contrasting description of American group life to that of Israel Zangwill. As Ned Landsman and Wendy Katkin pointed out in 1998, "*Beyond the Melting Pot* ... directly challenged the validity of the older, long-entrenched assimilationist paradigm for understanding group life in the United States" (Katkin, Landsman, and Tyree, *Beyond Pluralism*, 2). While the title of their book suggested that the age of the melting pot had been surpassed, in reality, the authors intended something different. As they outlined in their preface to the first edition of the book, "The notion that the intense and unprecedented mixture of ethnic and religious groups in American life was soon to blend into a homogeneous end product

---

1   For a helpful biographical sketch, see Berman, *Speaking of Jews: Rabbis, Intellectuals, and the Creation of an American Public Identity* (Berkeley: University of California Press, 2009): 102–109.

has outlived its usefulness, and also its credibility ... The point about the melting pot ... is that it did not happen" (Glazer and Moynihan, *Beyond the Melting Pot*, xcvii). The authors were not claiming simply that the age of the Melting Pot had passed; they were challenging the notion that it had ever existed. Put differently, "[t]hey did not mean that ethnics did not find a way to become American. They meant that becoming American did not necessitate discarding cultural particularity" (Greene, *The Jewish Origins*, 182). Most important of all, they had data to support their claims.

The New York City of 1963 that Glazer and Moynihan were describing was one that not only challenged the reality of Zangwill's melting pot, but also one that undermined Herberg's claim that the "triple melting pot" of American life exhibited itself in religious group identity rather than through ethnic ties. As the authors showed, New York City's diverse residents retained ethnic, national, *and* religious group ties that resulted in what Horace Kallen had called "hyphenated-Americans" many years prior. In the second edition of the book, published in 1970, Glazer and Moynihan went even further and claimed that, while in the original edition published seven years earlier "we argued that religion and race[2] seemed to be taking over from ethnicity ... in the last few years, the role of religion as a primary identity for Americans has weakened" (Glazer and Moynihan, *Beyond the Melting Pot*, xxxvi).[3] Their findings leveled a direct challenge both to Zangwill's notion that ethnic group identities would melt away and to Herberg's theory of America as a primarily religious triple melting pot. Considering the importance of their findings, Werner Sollors has written that "'Beyond the Melting Pot' was more than just the title of a book ... Its publication in 1963

---

2  Although race is no longer a credible scientific category, it was still very much in use in 1970. See, for example, Tracy Fessenden, "Race," in *Themes in Religions and American Culture*, eds. Philip Goff and Paul Harvey (Chapel Hill: The University of North Carolina Press, 2004): 129–161.

3  The categories of religion, race, and ethnicity are complex and overlapping. For a useful introduction to the issues related to these categories, see Philip Goff and Paul Harvey, eds. *Themes in Religion and American Culture* (Chapel Hill: The University of North Carolina Press, 2004).

marked the end of an era. It paved the way for the revival of American ethnic identification in the 1960s and 1970s ... " (Sollors, *Beyond Ethnicity*, 20). *Beyond the Melting Pot* began to describe what would, by the late 1980s, come to be known in the United States as multiculturalism.

More than 20 years after the publication of *Beyond the Melting Pot*, with ethnic revival well under way, Glazer authored the influential work, *We Are All Multiculturalists Now* (1997). Describing what he called "the multicultural explosion," Glazer presented an important overview of the rise of multiculturalism. As a theory of group life in America, multiculturalism is the next conceptual point along the twentieth-century arc. Glazer correctly observed that,

> Many terms have ... arisen to encompass the reality that groups of different origin all form part of the American population, and in varying degrees part of a common culture and society. Multiculturalism is just the latest in this sequence of terms describing how American society ... should respond to diversity." (Glazer, *We Are All Multiculturalists*, 8)

Like Kallen's cultural pluralism, multiculturalism rejected the notion of melting pot assimilation and affirmed fixed and distinct identities. As has been shown, Zangwill's melting pot idea implicated ethnic, national, and religious aspects of group identity and suggested that they would all melt away as newcomers would assimilate into American culture. While Kallen directed his attention to European ethnic and cultural identity groups, ignoring racial and religious ties, Herberg considered only religious categories of group identity. By contrast, multiculturalism addressed the full range of group identities. As a result, the net of multiculturalism has been cast more widely to include social groups based on gender and sexuality, as well as ethnicity and religion.[4] For multiculturalists, each one

---

4 Although some have suggested that "[t]he limit multiculturalism imposes on who will be recognized is set by the degree of prejudice and discrimination, or in stronger terms, 'oppression,' these groups have faced in the United States. Indeed, the opponents of multiculturalism label it 'oppression studies'" (Glazer, *We Are All*

represents a distinct culture that deserves to be included and protected in the United States. As such, the word "culture" in multiculturalism should be interpreted in the broadest sense of the term.

Although multiculturalism has a broader scope than does cultural pluralism, the similarities between the two theories are striking. The multicultural rejection of "assimilation and the 'melting pot' image as an imposition of the dominant culture" and its call for a society "in which each ethnic and racial element in the population maintains its distinctiveness" (Glazer, *We Are All Multiculturalists*, 10) meant that it shared a great deal in common with cultural pluralism in its prescriptions for the legitimacy and maintenance of group life and identity in America. As Glazer put it, the "new reality was once called cultural pluralism; it is now called multiculturalism" (Glazer, *We Are All Multiculturalists*, 97). Taking into account both the similarities and the differences between the two concepts, it would be more accurate to state, in agreement with David Hollinger, that "The 'cultural pluralism' associated with the name of Horace Kallen is an important precursor to multiculturalism" (Hollinger, *Postethnic America*, 11). In other words, multiculturalism continued the legacy of cultural pluralism in America, albeit in expanded form and by another name.

By the end of the twentieth century, cultural pluralism 2.0, now under the moniker of "multiculturalism," had become the most widely accepted, though still hotly contested,[5] group theory of the day. Crucially, multiculturalist thinking began to recognize the modifying effect of encounters in American society. Returning to *Beyond the Melting Pot*, Glazer and Moynihan recognized the "assimilating power of American society and culture [that] operated on immigrant groups in different ways, to make them … something they had not

---

*Multiculturalists*, 14). Nevertheless, even in light of this critique, multiculturalism does not discriminate between the varieties of group identities.

5  David Hollinger has written that multiculturalism is encumbered by the fact that "… its unifying principles have proved too vague to enable its adherents to sort out their own agreements and disagreements, and its vocabulary is not precise enough to parse the very different problems to which its followers look to it for help" (Hollinger, *Postethnic America*, 2).

been, but still something distinct and identifiable" (Glazer and Moynihan, *Beyond the Melting Pot*, 13–14). William Newman understood this to mean that "an Italian in Italy is different from an Italian-American ... Glazer and Moynihan explain how it is possible for both assimilation and cultural pluralism to have occurred in the United States" (Newman, *American Pluralism*, 79). Newman represented this modified brand of cultural pluralism mathematically in this form: $A + B + C = A^1 + B^1 + C^1$. In effect, multiculturalism described a reality in which different groups in American life could retain their distinct identities, while still feeling the influence of their exposure to "America" in all its diversity.

Writing almost 40 years after Kallen first articulated his theory of cultural pluralism, Glazer and Moynihan offered an updated version of his concept that accounted not only for the retention of distinct group identities, but also for the reality of social change, at least to some extent. Ultimately, however, multiculturalism also failed to capture the full extent of the changing nature of individual identity and group life in America.

The shortcomings of multiculturalism laid the groundwork for the final stop along the century-long arc of sociological theories of individual identity and group life in America. Historian David Hollinger published his influential work,[6] *Postethnic America: Beyond Multiculturalism*, in 1995, 80 years after Horace Kallen's groundbreaking essays in the pages of *The Nation* and *The Menorah Journal*. In an apparent nod to Glazer and Moynihan's title, *Beyond the Melting Pot*, the subtitle of Hollinger's book made the case for a move *Beyond Multiculturalism*[7] that extended past the ideas of Kallen, Herberg, and

---

6  Philip Gleason and Werner Sollors have written that Hollinger "has written a book that is analytically acute and morally courageous" (Gleason, "Review of Postethnic America," 1659) and that "Hollinger makes a convincing case, and I hope that his manifesto will be widely adopted" (Sollors, "Rev. of Postethnic America," 570).

7  Other scholars writing in the same field have employed similar titles. They include Werner Sollors, *Beyond Ethnicity: Consent and Descent in American Culture* (New York: Oxford University Press, 1986); Wendy F. Katkin, Ned Landsman, and Andrea Tyree, eds. *Beyond Pluralism: The Conception of Groups and Group Identities in America* (Urbana: University of Illinois Press, 1998); Chris Beneke, *Beyond Toleration: The Religious Origins of American Pluralism* (Oxford: Oxford University Press, 2006); and

the multiculturalists. Central to Hollinger's thesis was the question of how individuals become members of different social groups and the nature of the boundaries between them. As has been shown earlier, cultural pluralism, the triple melting pot, and multiculturalism each emphasized the importance of communities of descent and group boundaries. Postethnicity describes things differently.

Hollinger has written that "defenders of cultural diversity need to take a step beyond multiculturalism, toward a perspective I call 'postethnic'" (Hollinger, *Postethnic America*, 2–3). To draw out the meaning of postethnicity, Hollinger highlighted the tensions within multiculturalism. According to Hollinger, there are two streams of thought that flow within multiculturalist thinking; one pluralist, the other cosmopolitan. As he put it, "A postethnic perspective builds upon a cosmopolitan element prominent within the multiculturalist movement and cuts against its equally prominent pluralist element" (Hollinger, *Postethnic America*, 3). Contrasting Kallen's Cultural Pluralism with Randolph Bourne's[8] important ideas about cosmopolitanism, Hollinger drew a sharp distinction between the pluralist and cosmopolitan elements that are present within multiculturalist thinking. Hollinger described them in this way:

> Pluralism respects inherited boundaries and locates individuals within one or another of a series of ethno-racial groups to be protected or preserved. Cosmopolitanism is more wary of traditional enclosures and favors voluntary affiliations. Cosmopolitanism promotes multiple identities, emphasizes the dynamic and changing character of many groups, and is responsive to the potential for creating new cultural combinations. Pluralism sees in cosmopolitanism a threat to identity, while cosmopolitanism sees in pluralism a provincial unwillingness to engage the complex dilemmas

---

Courtney Bender and Pamela E. Klassen, eds. *After Pluralism: Reimagining Religious Engagement* (New York: Columbia University Press, 2010).

8  Randolph Bourne (1886–1918) was a progressive intellectual who was heavily influenced by Kallen. His 1916 essay, "Trans-National America" offered a rejection of the melting pot and outlined his vision for a cosmopolitan America.

and opportunities actually presented by contemporary life.
(Hollinger, *Postethnic America*, 3–4)

It is these four characteristics of cosmopolitanism—voluntary affiliations, or communities of assent (as opposed to descent); multiple identities; the dynamic and changing character of groups; and the potential for creating new cultural combinations—that Hollinger has emphasized in his theory of postethnicity.

Unlike Kallen's cultural pluralism, in which he failed to appreciate the implications of social encounters between individuals and across groups, postethnicity is predicated on the acknowledgment "that most individuals live in many circles simultaneously and that the actual living of any individual life entails a shifting division of labor between the several 'we's' of which the individual is a part" (Hollinger, *Postethnic America*, 106). In effect, and in stark contrast to cultural pluralism, the triple melting pot, and multiculturalism, postethnicity sees individuals as moving within and between identity groups of all kinds—ethno-racial,[9] cultural, religious, sexual, and so on—while having the capacity to identify with several at the same time.

It is helpful to consider the two planes upon which the "several we's" are experienced by Americans in the era of postethnicity. The first is the vertical plane and the second is the horizontal plane. The vertical axis relates to what Hollinger has called "communities of descent." To exemplify the complexity of communities of descent in postethnic America, Hollinger presented a powerful example. Referring to the 1976 Pulitzer prize–winning author of *Roots: The Saga of an American Family*, Hollinger quoted Ishmael Reed's observation that, "If Alex Haley had traced his father's bloodline, he would have travelled twelve generations back to, not Gambia, but Ireland . . . " (Hollinger, *Postethnic America*, 19). The point here was that even descent communities are more complex than Kallen understood, or wanted to believe. As Hollinger explained, " ... Haley could choose to identify with Africa ... [o]r Haley could choose to

---

9  This is Hollinger's term.

identify with Ireland ... postethnicity would enable Haley ... to be both African American and Irish American without having to choose one to the exclusion of the other" (Hollinger, *Postethnic America*, 20–21). In this reality, there is recognition of the complexity of communities of descent and that individuals can locate and identify with a variety of ancestral identities.

Taking it one step further, Hollinger suggested that communities of descent should not be thought of as determinative. As he has written, in direct contrast to Kallen,

> A Postethnic perspective challenges the right of one's grandfather or grandmother to determine primary identity. Individuals should be allowed to affiliate or disaffiliate with their own communities of descent to an extent that they choose, while affiliating with whatever nondescent communities are available and appealing to them. (Hollinger, *Postethnic America*, 116)

However, even as Hollinger claimed that identity is and should be voluntary, and that communities of descent should not determine one's affiliations, his theory of postethnicity did not call for a complete abandonment of inherited identity/ies. Recognizing that "many of the great cosmopolitans of history have been proudly rootless," Hollinger explained that, by contrast, "postethnicity is the critical renewal of cosmopolitanism in the context of today's greater sensitivity to roots" (Hollinger, *Postethnic America*, 5). This greater sensitivity is referred to as "rooted cosmopolitanism." In effect, "A postethnic perspective ... balances an appreciation for communities of descent with a determination to make room for new communities" (Hollinger, *Postethnic America*, 3). Whereas Kallen deemed communities of descent to be determinative, postethnicity honors their place, but only as part of what is a complex matrix of identity. As Shaul Magid has explained, rooted cosmopolitanism "is more respectful of ethnicity in principle but stresses voluntarism and not birth as the root of individual and collective identity" (Magid, *American*

*Post-Judaism*, 24). Communities of descent are neither the whole story nor are they beside the point. They are, according to Hollinger and Magid, part of the diverse range of voluntary identities available in postethnic America.

On the horizontal plane, postethnicity returns us to what happens "when peoples meet"—what I refer to as encounter. As we have seen, Kallen did not address the implications of social mixing between ethnic groups. In Kallen's vision of group life in America, families of singular European descent would live among their "kin" in specific geographic locales and be protected and defended by the law. All the while, interactions with members of other groups would be kept to a minimum, thus maintaining hyphenated American identities as purebred Italian-Americans, Jewish-Americans, or Polish-Americans, and so on. However, the reality for the last century has been far from Kallen's image. In postethnic America, social mixing is simply part of the warp and woof of life, resulting in a high volume of cross-group encounters and, as a result, in the adoption of hybrid identities.

It is to the "horizontal encounter" of postethnic America that I want to draw our focused attention. While multiculturalism (or modified cultural pluralism, as Newman called it) reflects an understanding that contact with "America" would result in a modified group identity (recall, $A + B + C = A^1 + B^1 + C^1$),[10] a postethnic orientation embraces the full impact of individual encounters, not just with "America" but, more important, with one another. As Peter Berger astutely observed in reference to Lubavitcher Hassidim many years prior, "All the individual has to do to get out of his alleged Jewish destiny is to walk out and take the subway. Outside, waiting, is the emporium of life-styles, identities, and religious preferences that constitutes American pluralism[11]" (Berger, *The Heretical Imperative*, 30). The metaphor of the emporium describes, in simple terms, the power of encounters on the horizontal plane.

---

10  See page 54.
11  Here, the term is simply a synonym for diversity.

Although his personal life confirmed this reality,[12] Horace Kallen's theoretical work did not account for the kind of cross-cultural encounters that take place, and increasingly so, on a daily basis in the lives of American citizens. As Courtney Bender and Pamela Klassen have pointed out with respect to religious identity, there are a "range of daily interactions and practices of translation, interpretation, and mutual indifference that shape the lived experience of religious diversity as a shared project in pluralistic ... societies" (Bender and Klassen, *After Pluralism*, 17). To take it one step further: these interactions not only shape the "lived experience" within diverse communities, they also result in a transformation of identity.

In his essay, "A Critique of Pure Pluralism" (1986), Werner Sollors described the power of encounter in postethnic terms almost a decade prior to Hollinger's publication of *Postethnic America*. Sollors articulated it in this way:

> The dominant assumption among serious scholars who study ethnic literature seems to be that history can be best written by separating the groups that produced such literature in the United States. The published results of this "mosaic" procedure are the readers and compendiums made up of diverse essays on groups of ethnic writers who may have little in common except so-called ethnic roots ... The contours of an ethnic literary history are beginning to emerge which views writers primarily as 'members' of various ethnic and gender groups. James T. Farrell may thus be discussed as a pure Irish-American writer, without any hint that he got interested in writing ethnic literature after

---

12 Kallen's own life reflected this complexity. He was a foreign-born child of Jewish immigrants who learned to navigate life as a Jew, albeit a secular one, at Harvard at the beginning of the twentieth century, where he was exposed to William James and George Santayana. These experiences, not to mention his marriage to Rachel Oatman Van Arsdale, a non-Jew, speak more to the realities and impact of encounter than to Kallen's notion of ethnic separatism.

> reading and meeting Abraham Cahan, and that his first stories were set in Polish-America—not to mention his interest in Russian and French writing or in Chicago sociology ... Taken exclusively, what is often called 'the ethnic perspective'—which often means, in literary history, the emphasis of a writer's descent—all but annihilates polyethnic art movements, moments of individual and cultural interaction, and the pervasiveness of cultural syncretism in America. (Sollors, "A Critique of Pure Pluralism," 255–256)

Here, Sollors described the shortcomings of both pluralist and multiculturalist thinking and suggested that literature and its authors cannot be easily compartmentalized as the products of singular descent communities. Supporting my central claim, Sollors identified the source of this new type of hybrid identity: the encounter. For example, Farrell's "polyethnic" writing was influenced by his "meeting Abraham Cahan" and the "moments of individual and cultural interaction" that made him so much more than solely an Irish-American author. While Kallen failed to appreciate the reality and implications of diverse human encounters and Glazer and Moynihan intuited their meaning but failed to recognize the full extent of their impact, Sollors appreciated the power of human encounters and recognized their outcome in the form of "cultural syncretism." As such, postethnicity is a more accurate description of this reality.

There is, of course, one form of encounter that has implications for both the vertical and horizontal planes: intermarriage. As David Biale has pointed out, "Intermarriage—an inevitability in an open society—has created individuals whose very being subverts any politics of monolithic identity" (Biale, "The Melting Pot and Beyond," 30). American society is one in which marriage—probably the most intense example of encounter between what Milton Gordon would call "primary relationships"—across cultural and ethnic groups, happens at an increasing rate and as a matter of course. One result is that the kind of cultural and ethnic purity that Kallen imagined is no longer possible (if it ever even existed in the first place). In situations in which intermarriage takes place, the partners in the marriage are horizontally influenced by their deep encounter with each other and the subsequent generations of offspring are influenced on the vertical plane by their culturally or ethnically diverse forebears.[13]

Turning to religious life in America, a postethnic trend resulting from encounters on the horizontal plane can be clearly identified. Scholars have noted the high rate of intermarriage between individuals with different religious affiliations and the impact it has had on religious identity. Robert Putnam and David Campbell devoted a chapter of their book, *American Grace: How Religion Divides and Unites Us* (2010), to the topic of "Switching, Matching, and Mixing." Appropriately, the subtitle of the chapter is "Inheriting versus Choosing Religion." The authors point out that "religious intermarriage rose steadily throughout the twentieth century to the point that today roughly half of all married Americans chose a partner from a different religious tradition" (Putnam and Campbell, *American Grace*, 160). Consistent with Hollinger's claims, Putnam and Campbell concluded that, as a result, "individual choice has become virtually as important as inheritance in explaining Americans' religious affiliations . . . " (Putnam and Campbell, *American Grace*, 160).[14]

In a postethnic reality, individuals encounter one another, leading them to reevaluate assumed identity/ies. As an expression of

---

13  For a useful analysis of the influence of intermarriage on identity, see Mary C. Waters, "Multiple Ethnic Identity Choices," Katkin, Wendy F., Ned Landsman, and Andrea Tyree, eds. *Beyond Pluralism: The Conception of Groups and Group Identities in America.* (Urbana: University of Illinois Press, 1998).

14  Although not entirely a result of increasing rates of intermarriage, it is also noteworthy that the 2015 Pew Research Center study, *America's Changing Religious Landscape*, showed that, with regard to "the three major Protestant traditions (evangelical Protestantism, mainline Protestantism, and historically black Protestantism) ... the share of Americans who have switched religions [is] 42%," and the percentage is even higher when all Americans are taken into consideration. This data simply underscores the extent to which individuals are shifting in their religious affiliations, or lack thereof, in the case of the rising number of "nones" (religiously unaffiliated adults).

affiliation, identity becomes fluid, resulting in porous boundaries between individuals and groups. In this reality, cultural, ethnic, or religious groups are no longer distinct instruments creating harmony by playing side by side in a larger symphony. Instead, individuals now move from instrument to instrument, playing different tunes, and creating new forms of music as they go. The result is less classical and more jazz fusion. In fact, the very instruments themselves are prone to being modified. To place postethnicity and cultural pluralism into stark relief, Hollinger rightly acknowledged that, "It may clarify the character and significance of these preferences to point out that none of them would have appealed to Horace Kallen" (Hollinger, *Postethnic America*, 116).

At the end of the century-long arc from Zangwill's melting pot to Hollinger's postethnicity, we might conclude that Glazer and Moynihan's claim that the melting pot never happened was premature. While the great crucible that David Quixano described in Zangwill's play certainly never materialized and immigrants to America never melted into a single, homogenous "new breed" of American, it is also the case that notions of "unmeltable ethnics"[15] that became popular in the 1970s were also wishful thinking. In the final analysis, postethnicity is closer to Zangwill's vision than it is to Kallen's. While Kallen's notion of cultural pluralism described clear and sharp boundaries between groups as both necessary (due to descent) and desirable (in the interests of democracy), Zangwill recognized that communities of descent did not have to be communities of destiny. In the end, Hollinger's description of America at the end of the twentieth century was more accurate—and increasingly so— than any of the theories that came before.

---

15 This phrase is taken from the title of Michael Novak's *Unmeltable Ethnics: Politics & Culture in American Life* (New York: Macmillan Publishing Company, 1972).

# PART II

## Chapter 5

## Greenberg Encounters the Holocaust

In Part I, the scene was set for an exploration of the development of Irving Greenberg's theology of Hybrid Judaism. The increasing denominationalism of American Jewry, the changing understanding and reality of religion in the United States, and the evolving sociology of identity all combined to create the conditions for Greenberg's work. Put differently, Greenberg's life and work can be thought of as a nexus for the various developments outlined in Part I.

Born in 1933, Greenberg was a child of immigrants who appeared in the midst of a rapidly changing American Jewish community. Coming of age in the years following the Second World War and the destruction of European Jewry, Greenberg was deeply concerned about the divisions within the Jewish community and threw himself into communal efforts to bring the leadership and the laity of the denominations closer together. As we shall see, he also engaged with the wider American religious landscape and was realistic about the complexity of religious affiliations in the modern world. Although he embraced the language of pluralism, his ideas moved beyond it to articulate a vision for American Jews that anticipated much of David Hollinger's theory of postethnicity and provided the theological basis for a more expansive understanding of religious identity.

While Greenberg is well known for his cross-denominational work with CLAL, The National Jewish Center for Learning and Leadership, and his passionate defense of *Shoah* memory, it is his postethnic theology of encounter—what I refer to as Hybrid Judaism—that stands as his most far-reaching contribution. Despite the attention of scholars,[1] the full implications of his theological system as a whole have eluded his readers. One reason for this is due to the fact that Greenberg's ideas are scattered across essays and monographs in a multitude of publications that span the better part of five decades.[2] It must also be emphasized that Greenberg arrived at his proto-postethnic theology of Hybrid Judaism over time. Although many of the ingredients of his theology were introduced in the 1960s, it would not be until much later that they would coalesce into a fully developed theology. What follows in Part II of this book is the first systematic treatment of Greenberg's unfolding theology of Hybrid Judaism.

In Part I, I presented Milton Gordon's critique that Horace Kallen's theory of cultural pluralism failed to consider what happens "when peoples meet."[3] Given the emphasis I have placed on the central importance of encounters in our understanding of identity, it should come as no surprise that Greenberg's theology is rooted in a set of personal experiences that must be considered if we are to understand it fully.[4] In Chapter 1, I surveyed some of the key encounters of Greenberg's early life: his father's example of respect for Conservative Judaism and Catholicism, his training as a student of history and *musar*, and his formative experiences at Harvard. These early experiences laid the groundwork for Greenberg's development as a boundary-breaking thinker and communal leader, but it would be the transformative encounters with non-Orthodox Jews and non-Jews during his adult life that

---

1   As noted earlier, the focus of almost all of the scholarly attention paid to Greenberg's work has been narrowly focused on his Holocaust theology. See Introduction, footnote 10.

2   Although Greenberg has yet to produce a systematic theological tract that lays out the full extent of his thinking, he has been working on a magnum opus theological work for a number of years.

3   See pp. 42-43.

4   Greenberg also recognized the importance of encounter, using the term often. See, for example, Irving Greenberg, "The New Encounter of Judaism and Christianity." *Barat Review* 3, no. 2 (1967): 113–125; *For the Sake of Heaven and Earth: The New Encounter between Judaism and Christianity* (Philadelphia: The Jewish Publication Society, 2004); and "A Lifetime of Encounters with the Rav." *The Commentator*, 2007.

would provide the generative force for his theology of Hybrid Judaism.

In 1961, Greenberg took leave of his post as professor of history at Yeshiva University and served as a Fulbright visiting lecturer at Tel Aviv University. During this time, Greenberg had what was probably the most significant encounter of his life, this time not with a person, but rather with a historical event. He has described it as "an explosive confrontation with the Holocaust" (Greenberg, *For the Sake of Heaven and Earth*, 5). As a child, Greenberg had only limited exposure to the Holocaust. As he has written,

> Without talking about the Holocaust openly, my parents had communicated in muffled—but deep—ways that something terrible had happened. My mother had lost five of her seven brothers; all five had stayed behind in Poland, together with their entire families, just as my father had lost one sister and her family who did not come to this country. I have dim memories, from World War II and after, of my mother crying in her room, away from the children—but we did not talk about the catastrophe openly. (Greenberg, *For the Sake of Heaven and Earth*, 6)

In addition to the experiences of his extended family, Greenberg also had teachers that had lived through the Holocaust. Referring to the faculty at Beth Joseph Rabbinical Seminary, where he studied while an undergraduate at Brooklyn College, Greenberg remembered that "half were survivors of the camps, and a third were survivors from Siberia" (Freedman, *Living in the Image of God*, 3). However, like many other children growing up in the United States during and immediately after the war years, Greenberg did not confront the full reality of the Holocaust until much later.[5]

5 For a thorough discussion of the extent to which the Holocaust was discussed publicly in the American Jewish community in the years immediately following the end of the war, see Hasia R. Diner, *We Remember with Reverence and Awe: American Jews and the Myth of Silence after the Holocaust, 1945–1962* (New York: New York

Initially, the Holocaust was not central to Greenberg's thinking. As he described his initial time in Israel: "The week we arrived in the capital [Jerusalem] was the last week of the Eichmann trial, and an acquaintance offered to help me gain admission to the trial. I declined because we were not settled in yet. Honestly, such a direct encounter with the *Shoah* was not my highest priority." However, "Within a few weeks after passing up a chance to attend the Eichmann trial, I was caught up in a frenzy about the Holocaust" (Greenberg, *For the Sake of Heaven and Earth*, 5–6). It is worth quoting Greenberg at length to understand the full impact of his encounter with the horrors of the Holocaust:

> Soon the encounter with the *Shoah* took over my days and nights … other than the hours in which I prepared for classes, I spent all my time reading about the Holocaust … increasingly, my time was spent at Yad Vashem[6] … In the winter, the building was cold; but the chill in my soul was icier. The grip of death and destruction penetrated and froze me to the bone. Shock followed shock. Outrage, humiliation, and fear took over, and soon my religious life was invaded by tormenting doubts and moral revulsion … I was drowning religiously … There were mornings when I would put on my tefillin and then sit there, overwhelmed by the horrifying sights and disturbing sounds from *Shoah* sources that flashed through my mind, unable to recite the words of the siddur. (Greenberg, *For the Sake of Heaven and Earth*, 6–7)

The impact of his encounter with the historical reality and tragedy of the Holocaust was immediate and transformative. Upon his return to the United States, and as a direct response to his revelation about the Holocaust, Greenberg committed himself to "do more Jewishly" (Freedman, *Living in the Image of God*, 10). He determined to offer one of the first college-level courses ever taught on the subject of the

---

University Press, 2009), and David Cesarani and Eric J. Sundquist, eds. *After the Holocaust: Challenging the Myth of Silence* (New York: Routledge, 2012).

6  The Holocaust memorial museum in Jerusalem.

Holocaust.[7] In the years and decades that followed, his commitment to Holocaust memory intensified. In 1975, he established a Holocaust memorial organization—*Zachor*: Holocaust Resource Center—with Elie Wiesel[8] and, from 1979 to 1980, served as the first director of President Jimmy Carter's Commission on the Holocaust. The commission would ultimately lead to the establishment of the United States Holocaust Memorial Museum in Washington, DC, of which Greenberg would serve as chairman from 2000 to 2002.[9]

Greenberg's transformative experience in Israel in 1961 also influenced his thinking about the American Jewish community. In 1965, just a few years after his Fulbright fellowship, Greenberg went on the record stating that denominations had limited utility and that there was "ambiguity in all of these groupings" ("Toward Jewish Religious Unity," 153). Confirming the increasingly important role of the Holocaust in his thinking, he declared that "I personally feel that after Auschwitz we should be embarrassed to use the words 'Orthodox,' 'Conservative,' or 'Reform'" ("Toward Jewish Religious Unity," 156).[10] Although it would take years for Greenberg to fully unpack the meaning of this claim—a process that would eventually de-center the Holocaust's place in his theology—it will suffice to state for now that responding to his own realization of the extent of the tragedy of the Holocaust was both the starting point for his commitment to Jewish communal work and the orienting event in the development of his thinking.

---

7  Greenberg recalled that, following his return from Israel, "After a two-year fight, I won the right to teach about the Holocaust (although I had to promise to teach the course under a different title: 'Totalitarianism and Ideology in the 20th Century')" (Freedman, *Living in the Image of God*, 10).

8  Elie Wiesel (1928–2016) was a Holocaust survivor, author, and Nobel Laureate. Greenberg played a significant role in Wiesel's life. In a festschrift in honor of Greenberg's 75th birthday, Wiesel wrote that, "were it not for you, my entire academic life would not have been what it is" (Katz and Bayme, *Continuity and Change*, 277).

9  For an excellent analysis of the establishment of the President's Commission and the founding of the Museum, see Edward T. Linenthal, *Preserving Memory: The Struggle to Create America's Holocaust Museum* (New York: Columbia University Press, 2001).

10  This appears to be the earliest published formulation of Greenberg's oft-quoted quip that "it doesn't matter what denomination you are, as long you are ashamed of it."

Greenberg's first public exploration of these ideas took place at a gathering of the Orthodox student group, Yavneh. Historian Benny Kraut has described Yavneh as "an independent Orthodox student-run national collegiate organization" (Kraut, *The Greening of American Orthodoxy*, 20) that was founded in early 1960. Greenberg was present at the organization's first convention and served as chair of its National Advisory Board from 1960 to 1966. His first published essay was the text of a speech he delivered at the organization's third annual national convention in 1962. A self-professed Greenberg devotee, Kraut[11] recalled that, "The speech he delivered to the third annual national Yavneh convention September 2, 1962, 'Yavneh: Looking Ahead, Values and Goals,' with idealistic passion outlined a blueprint for future Yavneh activities" (Kraut, *The Greening of American Orthodoxy*, 41). The text of the speech appeared in the fall of 1962 in the pages of the first edition of the journal *Yavneh Studies: A Jewish Collegiate Publication*. Already, in this very first essay, when he was just 29 years of age, Greenberg addressed head on the question of intra-Jewish relations in light of the Holocaust.

The essay opened with a tantalizing question: "Have you ever wondered what would happen if Mashiach [the messiah] came?" (Greenberg, "Yavneh," 46). After a whimsical and somewhat cynical narrative describing the presumed responses to the arrival of the messiah,[12] Greenberg suggested that, in all seriousness, "We are living in Messianic times yet our motto seems to be 'business as usual'" (Greenberg, "Yavneh," 47). According to him, the arrival of the messi-

---

11  In the "Personal Postscript" to his history of Yavneh, Kraut noted that he was "infused with the vital effervescent spirit of Irving Greenberg" (Kraut, *The Greening of American Orthodoxy*, 167).

12  For example, Greenberg wrote:

> Ed Sullivan wires an offer of a $50,000 fee for exclusive rights for the first appearance of Mashiach on television ... After an all night session of the Ecumenical Council, chaired by the Pope and closed to the press, the Vatican announces the following decision of the Church: 'The reputed Messiah is to be stopped at once and asked the following question: Is this his first or second coming? If it is his second, he is to be allowed to proceed and greeted with hosannas in Jerusalem. If it is his first, he is a fraud. (Greenberg, "Yavneh," 46–47)

anic era was the result of two historical events that resulted in the destruction of traditional European Jewish life. The first event was "the Emancipation and westernization which washed away the Torah centered community framework of our life as a people" (Greenberg, "Yavneh," 47) and the second event, even more crucial to the arrival of the messianic era, was the tragic destruction of European Jewry. Referring to " ... World War II and the extermination of six million Jews ... " Greenberg inquired, "I wonder if you realize what a watershed this experience is in our lives." The result of this historical event, according to Greenberg, was that "It has demolished all our established conventional positions and put us under the stern necessity of rebuilding our lives—if we are courageous enough to face up to it honestly ... " (Greenberg, "Yavneh," 47). The original text includes the ellipsis at the end of the sentence, as if to communicate that there were not enough words, or that Greenberg had not yet arrived at how to describe this new, post-Holocaust, proto-messianic reality.

Offering a strident critique of modernity, Greenberg claimed that the Holocaust had "revealed the bankruptcy and insufficiency of Western civilization by itself and shown up its claim of moral progress and that man was being perfected by modern culture ... Tragically enough it has taken this catastrophe to give us insight into the limitations of contemporary civilization" (Greenberg, "Yavneh," 47). Despite the human tragedy of the Holocaust and Greenberg's suspicions about the post-Enlightenment world that did little to prevent it, he did not respond with complete rejection. Instead, he wrote that, "We, the survivors,[13] now have to work out a new relationship of communication with a culture whose goodness and achievement we appreciate but whose evil and limitations we have experienced" (Greenberg, "Yavneh," 47). In no uncertain terms, Greenberg described the implications of these events and this new realization:

> It has radically changed being a Jew—even for the assimilated. Being Jewish is no longer merely a discrimination or

---

13  Greenberg used this terminology to refer to all Jews living in the post-Holocaust era.

disadvantage one is born into. It is a serious identification for which a person may have to die [God forbid] ... The point is that every Jew must now face up to the fact and ask himself: is it worth it? He must make something of it or face the ultimate absurdity of risking his life for something meaningless to him. (Greenberg, "Yavneh," 47–48)

In these words, Greenberg declared that the advent of modernity and the Holocaust presented nothing less than an existential challenge to the Jewish identity of those that were living in their aftermath.

He concluded his Yavneh essay with the assurance that,

If we will only see the true condition of our times and grow to meet the challenge, then we will be for all time the generation of rebirth and redemption. Then mankind will know that in our times too,
while evil men were engaged in destruction;
while foolish men were engaged in business as usual;
while the world was engaged in crisis and fear,
The Holy One, Blessed be He, was engaged in preparing the light of Mashiach.[14] (Greenberg, "Yavneh," 53)

Ultimately, Greenberg saw a coming redemption in spite of the spiritual destruction of Jewish life that resulted from the European Emancipation and the human destruction of the Holocaust. Rather than retreat from western civilization, Greenberg called for "a new relationship" and urged the Jewish community "to meet the challenge."

In the intervening pages of the Yavneh essay, Greenberg outlined what he believed it would take to realize the messianic promise of

---

14  The text is formatted this way in the original.

the moment. Speaking at the Yavneh convention meant that Greenberg was addressing Orthodox students predominantly on secular college campuses. Having established the grave importance of modernity and the Holocaust as defining historical events, he turned to their meaning for those in attendance. Focusing on the Holocaust, Greenberg claimed that there were now three "entirely new dimensions to being an Orthodox Jew" (Greenberg, "Yavneh," 48). The first addressed the nature of the relationship with God, the second turned to the Jewish understanding of history, and the third related to his audience's contemporary Jewish community.

Beginning with the first "new dimension," Greenberg wrote that the Holocaust "has revolutionized our relationship with G-d" and asked "How can we serve Him conventionally ever again? How can we bear the infinite weight of the sorrow of our brothers?" (Greenberg, "Yavneh," 48). Greenberg's answer was that "the revival must start with learning, for Torah is the source of living contact with G-d and His rejuvenating holiness" (Greenberg, "Yavneh," 49). In practical terms, Greenberg identified Yavneh's mandate as an organization for the furtherance of Jewish education as a direct response to the Holocaust.

Turning to the second "new dimension to being an Orthodox Jew," Greenberg highlighted the pain and destruction of the Holocaust and declared that

> It has challenged us to broaden our philosophy and understanding of Torah. We simply dare not shut out a single Jewish experience from our understanding. Can we embrace the agony and suffering of six million Jews? Can we keep them alive? Can we find balm for their wounds and cover their nakedness with our love? If we fail [God forbid], only then will they die again and finally. The experience of every one of them—the Tsaddik,[15] the Bundist, the Zionist

---

15  The Hasidic Master.

and the assimilationist, the moral and the mean, must be incorporated into our understanding of Jewish history and seen in their pointing the way to the Kingdom of G-d. (Greenberg, "Yavneh," 48)

Here, Torah and history are deployed as synonyms, alerting the listener/reader to Greenberg's belief in the seamless connection between history and theology. This will become a central aspect of Greenberg's unfolding tri-stage covenantal theology.[16] For now, Greenberg described the sacred responsibility of the Orthodox community to expand its understanding of Torah[17] to include every variety of Jew that perished in the Holocaust as "pointing the way to the Kingdom of G-d" (Greenberg, "Yavneh," 48). After the Holocaust, the old religious world of isolation and excommunication would not suffice.

Greenberg drew support from classical sources to make his case for a new Torah/history that would encompass "the Tsaddik, the Bundist, the Zionist and the assimilationist." In these texts, Greenberg identified a precedent for a more expansive "Torah" by their inclusion of a diversity of characters. As he put it,

The lives of the Fathers[18] and the behavior of the Meraglim[19]; the happiness of Purim and the suffering of Tisha B'Av[20] – all must be seen in the framework of divine pattern. The behavior of Avraham and the behavior of Lot – by showing what is right and showing what is wrong – must be understood. (Greenberg, "Yavneh," 48)

---

16  See pp. 86-88.
17  Here, "Torah" refers not to the Five Books of Moses, but rather to the more expansive sense of the Orthodox religious worldview.
18  The biblical patriarchs from the book of Genesis: Abraham, Isaac, and Jacob.
19  The biblical spies that were sent by Moses to survey the land of Canaan. See Numbers 13:1–14:45.
20  The ninth of Av—the annual fast day that commemorates the destruction of the first and second Temple in Jerusalem.

Here, Greenberg staked out poles of right and wrong by contrasting the biblical patriarchs with the spies in the desert, the joyous celebration of Purim with the mournful commemoration of the destruction of the Temple on the ninth of Av, and the hospitality of Abraham with his nephew Lot's misadventure in Sodom. Implicit in his claim was the suggestion that some among "the Tsaddik, the Bundist, the Zionist and the assimilationist" were comparable to the spies, Tisha B'Av, and Lot (all negative representations). Despite the not-yet-pluralistic and rather simplistic duality in these associations, Greenberg's larger point was that, after the Holocaust, Orthodox Jews needed to be more inclusive rather than less so.

Greenberg perceived in the tragic events of the Holocaust the moral imperative to acknowledge those who were murdered, regardless of their particular Jewish attachments (or lack thereof), and to include them in the sacred religio-historical narrative of the Jewish people. By doing so, survivors of the Holocaust could save those who were murdered from total demise. Realizing the enormity of this responsibility, he acknowledged that "Someone jokingly told me that in view of Yavneh's goals of Jewish study and excellence in college, of professional growth and maturity, of revitalizing Judaism and Jewish life, each member would have to live seven lives" (Greenberg, "Yavneh," 52). Responding seriously, Greenberg wrote that, "Ever since I have seen the full tragedy of our people, I have believed that this is true. Every Jew must live not only for himself, but for the little children who never were given a chance to grow up. We must experience deeply for the millions who were not allowed to do so" (Greenberg, "Yavneh," 52). For Greenberg, the events of the Holocaust meant that survivors had to live their lives on behalf of those that had perished.

In his third and final "new dimension to being an Orthodox Jew," Greenberg turned from the past to his contemporary Jewish reality. He wrote that,

we must relate ourselves anew to non-religious Jews who—
it took Hitler to remind and teach us—are our brothers in

life and in death. The knowledge of our common destiny must prevent us from abandoning them or self righteously writing them off. It must spur us until we bind our lives to theirs and draw them with bands of love and sympathy ever closer to Torah. (Greenberg, "Yavneh," 48)

Here, we have Greenberg's first explicit prescription regarding the nature of the post-Holocaust relationship between Orthodox Jews and the rest of the Jewish community. In this call for unity as a response to the Holocaust, Greenberg reminded his listeners/readers that they shared a "common destiny" with non-Orthodox Jews and cautioned them not to "self righteously write them off." Moreover, Greenberg entreated his Orthodox audience not to abandon the non-Orthodox community and instead "draw them with bands of love and sympathy ever closer to Torah," echoing the mishnaic statement attributed to Hillel that Jews should act like the disciples of Aaron and "love peace, pursue peace, love our fellow creatures and draw them closer to Torah."[21] Greenberg continued, "Who among us will help us understand how Mashiach is being brought closer by the very apikoros[22] who is stripping a Jewish teenager of his tradition and turning him into a secular idealist or, all too often, into a street corner 'hood'?" (Greenberg, "Yavneh," 49).[23] Again, Greenberg displayed the early vintage of these ideas when he implied that non-Orthodox Jews were heretics and that they were "far from Torah." Nevertheless, he also affirmed non-Orthodox Jews as partners in the *telos* of Jewish history.

Notwithstanding its shortcomings, Greenberg's Yavneh speech still stands as a visionary statement that ultimately called on its audience "to restore the broken unity and wholeness of Israel" (Greenberg,

---

21  Mishnah Avot 1:12.

22  Heretic.

23  In this comment, Greenberg cited Rabbi Abraham Isaac Kook's (1865–1935) magnum opus work, *Lights of the Holy* (in Ben Zion Bokser, ed., *Abraham Isaac Kook: The Lights of Penitence, Lights of Holiness, The Moral Principles, Essays, Letters, and Poems.* Mahwah: Paulist Press, 1978) hinting at the influence of Kook's writings on his thinking (Freedman, *Living in the Image of God*, 272).

"Yavneh," 49). It also made clear that his early thinking was inclined toward greater inclusivity of the full breadth of the Jewish community. Perceiving nothing less than a messianic outcome, Greenberg drew on traditional midrashic sources[24] to remind his readers that "at all times when disaster has been met by unquenchable Jewish will to rebuild, G-d has been there 'engaged in preparing the light of the Mashiach'" (Greenberg, "Yavneh," 49). For him, Yavneh had a critical role to play in the rebuilding of Jewish life after the Holocaust. The very name of the organization represented an explicit identification with the legendary center of learning that developed in the town of Yavneh (Jamnia) in the wake of the Roman destruction of the Second Temple in Jerusalem in the first century of the Common Era. In Greenberg's words, "Then, too, at a time of terrible destruction, the seeds of rebirth were planted … We believe that now, as then, the revival must start with learning" (Greenberg, "Yavneh," 49). For Greenberg, the Jewish rebirth and revival following the Holocaust needed to begin with a program of Jewish educational activities that would be led by the Yavneh membership.[25]

In his association of the Holocaust and the advent of modernity with the destruction of the second Temple in Jerusalem, Greenberg suggested that these modern events also represented a historical and theological rupture.[26] In similar fashion to the rabbinic tradition that interpreted the destruction of the second temple as representing a historical and theological turning point for the Jewish people, Greenberg understood modernity and the Holocaust as representing another momentous shift. This claim would be the basis of much of his work for the next 50 years; any comprehensive understanding of Greenberg's work must be attentive to this central point.

---

24  Specifically, *Genesis Rabba*, ch. 85.

25  For a detailed description of the educational program, see Benny Kraut, *The Greening of American Orthodox Judaism: Yavneh in the 1960s* (Cincinnati: Hebrew Union College Press, 2011): 35–75.

26  Elsewhere, Greenberg has referred to the rupture as an "orienting experience," a "*touchstone* of theology," and a "*ceasura.*" See Irving Greenberg, "Theology after the Shoah: The Transformation of the Core Paradigm." *Modern Judaism* 26, no. 3 (October 2006): 213–239.

Ultimately, each of Greenberg's major contributions to Jewish thought and communal upbuilding in the subsequent half century since the publication of the Yavneh essay have represented his further attempts to respond, as an American Jew, to the advent of modernity and the horrors of the Holocaust. In this, his very first publication, the influence of these events on his thinking is unmistakable. The Yavneh essay also reflected the early vintage of Greenberg's thinking with regard to intra-group relations in the Jewish community. Although he was not yet using the language of pluralism, this essay is clearly the starting point for an understanding of Greenberg's thinking on the subject. As Benny Kraut has rightly observed, the Yavneh speech "foreshadowed Greenberg's own future Torah-centered but pluralist agenda, which he later took with him to CLAL (National Jewish Center for Learning and Leadership) and other institutional settings" (Kraut, *The Greening of American Orthodoxy*, 41). One of these settings was the Christian–Jewish dialogue movement; it is to that topic that we now turn.

# Chapter 6

# Dialogue: Greenberg's Christian Influences

In trying to understand the meaning and implications of the Holocaust, Greenberg extended his attention beyond just the Jewish community and engaged with thinkers and activists in the Christian world. As Greenberg has recalled, following their year in Israel in 1961, "Blu [Greenberg's wife][1] and I decided that upon our return to America we would join the Jewish–Christian dialogue" (Greenberg, *For the Sake of Heaven and Earth*, 8). The goal was clear: "We felt that the only way Christianity would change its traditional 'teaching of contempt' for Judaism and Jewry would be if the dialogue dealt with theology" (Greenberg, *For the Sake of Heaven and Earth*, 14). As a result, Greenberg became an influential participant in the growing Christian–Jewish dialogue movement that developed in the late 1960s and early 1970s.[2]

His involvement in the Christian–Jewish dialogue movement brought Greenberg into direct disagreement with Joseph B. Soloveitchik, the head of Yeshiva University's Rabbi Isaac Elchanan Theological Seminary (RIETS) and the unofficial leader of Modern Orthodoxy in the United States. In 1964, Soloveitchik published an

---

1 Blu Greenberg (1936– ) has also played a significant role in the American Jewish community. A published author and poet, Greenberg has been the most influential force in the Orthodox feminist movement since its founding in the early 1970s.

2 The term "Christian" refers to Protestant Christianity. Of course, Catholic-Jewish dialogue was well under way due to the opening of the Second Vatican Council by Pope John XXIII, in 1962. The council concluded its work in 1965, under the leadership of Pope John VI, with the issuance of *Nostra Aetate*, which reversed the centuries-old charge of deicide at the hands of all Jews.

essay entitled "Confrontation," in which he laid out his position that Christians and Jews could come together to address shared communal interests, but that dialogue around theology and doctrine was out of bounds. In his words, "The relationship between the two communities must be ... related to the secular orders with which men come face to face. In the secular sphere, we may discuss positions to be taken, ideas to be evolved, and plans to be formulated" (Soloveitchik, "Confrontation," 24). Although he never publicly confronted Soloveitchik, by engaging in Christian–Jewish dialogue and thereby contradicting the ruling of his mentor, Greenberg challenged standard Orthodox practice and the leader of his own religious community.

As an increasingly active member of the Christian–Jewish dialogue movement, Greenberg was a regular attendee at its conferences and gatherings. In 1970, in a story it ran under the headline "A Dialogue of the Faiths at Seton Hall," *The New York Times* noted Greenberg's partic-ipation and included a large image of him in serious contemplation at a meeting of Christian and Jewish theologians discussing the meaning of the State of Israel for the field of theology. Then, in 1974, Greenberg participated in the International Symposium on the Holocaust, held at the Cathedral of St. John the Divine, in New York City. His influential paper, "Cloud of Smoke, Pillar of Fire: Judaism, Christianity, and Modernity after the Holocaust," was published in the 1977 collection of the conference papers, *Auschwitz: Beginning of a New Era?* In it, Greenberg presented a harrowing and detailed description of the horrors of the Holocaust and their theological implications. The chapter established him as a leading Holocaust theologian alongside the likes of Eliezer Berkovits, Emil Fackenheim, Richard Rubenstein, and Elie Wiesel.[3] It also positioned him as a leading figure in the growing Christian–Jewish dialogue movement.[4]

---

3  For an excellent introduction to the full breadth of Holocaust theology, see Steven T. Katz, Shlomo Biderman, and Gershon Greenberg, eds. *Wresting with God: Jewish Theological Responses during and after the Holocaust.* (Oxford: Oxford University Press, 2007).

4  Of course, Greenberg was neither the first nor the only active participant in the dialogue movement. For example, prior to his involvement, Abraham Joshua

Although Greenberg intended to influence Christian thinking, he did not anticipate that his own thinking would also change as a result of his encounters in the Christian–Jewish dialogue. In the end, his understanding of both Judaism and Christianity would be transformed. As Marc A. Krell has pointed out, "Greenberg is one of the first twentieth-century Jewish theologians to attempt a reconfiguration of Jewish and Christian identities that takes into account their historical and theological interdependence" (Krell, *Intersecting Pathways*, 129–130). The source of this reconfiguration was undoubtedly Greenberg's direct and sustained encounter with Christian thinkers who were also grappling with the meaning of the Holocaust for Christianity.[5] In particular, Greenberg became close friends with Alice and Roy Eckardt,[6] with whom he and his wife, Blu, partnered to further the Christian–Jewish dialogue movement, with a particular focus on the theological legacy of the Holocaust.

A breakthrough in Greenberg's thinking occurred in 1976 when "Zachor, the Holocaust Research Center branch of CLAL, ran a conference for Jewish and Christian scholars titled 'The Work of Elie Wiesel and the Holocaust Universe.'" (Greenberg, *For the Sake of Heaven and Earth*, 26). Reflecting back on the conference, Greenberg has written that "one paper jolted me to the core: Roy Eckardt's 'The Recantation of the Covenant?'" (Greenberg, *For the Sake of Heaven and Earth*, 26). Eckardt claimed that, because the Holocaust was the

---

Heschel (1907–1972) and Marc H. Tanenbaum (1925–1992) played key roles during the Second Vatican Council. For an introduction to the fullness of the Christian–Jewish dialogue movement, see Eugene J. Fisher, A. James Rudin, and Marc H. Tanenbaum, *Twenty Years of Jewish–Catholic Relations* (New York: Paulist Press, 1986); Edward J. Bristow, *No Religion is an Island: The Nostra Aetate Dialogues* (New York: Fordham University Press, 1998); and Tikva Frymer-Kensky, David Novak, Peter Ochs, David Fox Sandmel, and Michael A. Signer, eds. *Christianity in Jewish Terms* (Boulder: Westview Press, 2000).

5 See Marc A. Krell, *Intersecting Pathways: Modern Jewish Theologians in Conversation with Christianity* (Oxford: Oxford University Press, 2003): 103–130.

6 Arthur Roy Eckardt (1918–1998), professor of Religion at Lehigh University and a clergyman of the United Methodist Church, was a leading figure in the Christian–Jewish dialogue movement. Alice Eckardt (1923– ) is Professor Emerita of Religious Studies at Lehigh University and was also a significant figure in the Christian–Jewish dialogue movement.

price the Jews paid for being party to the covenant with God, "the only acceptable *teshuvah* [repentance] for God would be to recant the divine covenant and thus remove the Jews from the extreme danger they were in" (Greenberg, *For the Sake of Heaven and Earth*, 26). The impact of Eckardt's thinking on Greenberg was profound: "That night, I tossed and turned in my bed, blistered by the searing force of Eckardt's statement … " (Greenberg, *For the Sake of Heaven and Earth*, 26–27). After what Greenberg has described as years of searching, "at last I came to a realization that reconciled the conflicts that were tearing me apart. Roy Eckardt was absolutely right … But his prophetic insight was 'off' in one way. The Abrahamic–Sinaitic covenant was not finished—but the *commanded stage of the covenant* had come to its end" (Greenberg, *For the Sake of Heaven and Earth*, 27). Greenberg's profound encounter with Eckardt through the Christian–Jewish dialogue movement had led him to one of his most significant theological innovations.

Greenberg's participation in the Christian–Jewish dialogue not only influenced the development of his own covenantal theology, it also transformed his understanding and appreciation of Christianity. As Protestant theologians struggling to understand the meaning of the Holocaust, the Eckardts offered an impassioned critique of Christianity. For Greenberg, "Their model broke through my neat categories" and "thanks to them, I began to vicariously grasp the Christian worldview and experience it without the covert assumptions of superiority and moral judgment that were endemic in Jewish tradition" (Greenberg, *For the Sake of Heaven and Earth*, 19). In fact, Greenberg had become so sympathetic to Christianity that, by 1986, he would write that

> The rabbis concluded that Christianity is an alien growth, developed by those who followed a false Messiah. The rabbis perhaps erred here … Out of defensiveness, the rabbis confused a 'failed' Messiah (which is what Jesus was) and a false Messiah. A false Messiah is one who has the wrong values … A failed messiah is one who has the right values, upholds the covenant, only did not attain the final

goal. (Greenberg, "The Relationship of Judaism and Christianity," 201)

Greenberg's claim represented a radical new appraisal of Jesus from a Jewish perspective and invited the ire of many in the Orthodox community. Recalling the reactions to his claim, Greenberg wrote that

> to grant any pluralist legitimacy to Christianity was beyond the pale for most Orthodox colleagues … this latest development added incendiary fuel to the Orthodox community's smoldering anger at my public validations of the Conservative and Reform movements … taken together, my interfaith actions and this new denunciation led to my being brought up on charges of heresy and violation of Orthodox disciplines before my rabbinic organization, the Rabbinical Council of America. (Greenberg, *For the Sake of Heaven and Earth*, 33)

Although the heresy charges were dropped and no punitive action was taken,[7] Greenberg was still assailed in the pages of the Orthodox Union's magazine, *Jewish Action*.[8] Given the opportunity to refute claims that he had accepted Jesus as the messiah, Greenberg accepted the invitation to reply to the accusations.[9] Due to his concern that readers would have "no familiarity with the subtleties of thought in this subject," Greenberg confessed

---

7 There are no public records of the proceedings and even Greenberg has acknowledged that "To this day, I do not know all that transpired behind the scenes" (Greenberg, *For the Sake of Heaven and Earth*, 34).

8 It is noteworthy that the author of the attack on Greenberg was Hillel Goldberg, the same individual who, more than 20 years earlier, conducted the interview that was published in the pages of *The Commentator*. See Chapter 8, The Open Society. See also Hillel Goldberg, "An Orthodox Spokesman to Non-Orthodox Jewry: Is the Message Authentic?" *Jewish Action*. (Fall 5751/1990): 82–87.

9 See Irving Greenberg, "On the Relationship of Jews and Christians and of Jews and Jews." *Jewish Action* (Winter 5751/1990-199): 20, 22–24, 26, 28. For Goldberg's response, see Hillel Goldberg, "Rejoinder." *Jewish Action* (Winter 5751/1990–1991): 29–34.

many years later that he "had no choice but to explain away any possibility that my thinking was in any way Christological. In the end, I was forced to play down many of the innovative appreciations and nuanced theological insights that I had attributed to Christianity" (Greenberg, *For the Sake of Heaven and Earth*, 34). Although Greenberg felt straitened by political considerations, leading him to downplay the influence of Christianity on his thinking, nothing could have been farther from the truth. As Greenberg recalled, "I minimized the original and daring elements in the essay, stressing the most palatable interpretations that would cause the least dissonance in the Orthodox community" (Greenberg, *For the Sake of Heaven and Earth*, 34). Even though at the time Greenberg felt obliged to soften the full extent of his ideas in public, years later he would write that, "despite what had just happened, I still dreamt of reshaping the Orthodox community, hoping to regain its understanding and help move it back toward the rest of the Jewish community and towards Christians and society at large" (Greenberg, *For the Sake of Heaven and Earth*, 34). In these retrospective admissions, Greenberg acknowledged that his claims *were* radical and that, despite his retractions, he was deeply influenced by Christian theology. Although Greenberg's critics were mistaken in the full extent of their accusation (he never made any claim to the messiahship of Jesus), it was certainly the case that he was engaging in much more than simple interfaith ecumenism.

One way of understanding this controversy from the perspective of Greenberg's accusers is that they viewed his ideas from the perspective of Cultural Pluralists. From their point of view, religious groups should have distinct boundaries and steer clear of each other, except when absolutely necessary to maintain social harmony. Given this worldview, Greenberg clearly had crossed a line and needed reigning in. From Greenberg's proto-postethnic perspective, however, he was simply negotiating the open society, and living up to his own theology of encounter. To be clear, Greenberg would surely deny, in all sincerity, that he was both a Jew and a Christian. At the same time, the very designations "Jew" and "Christian" represent a cultural pluralist set of distinctions that may no longer be useful in postethnic America. While Greenberg has always self-identified with the Orthodox community, his theology also reflects the deep influences of both the non-Orthodox and non-Jewish worlds. For him, nothing less could be desirable in the age of encounter.

Returning to Greenberg's covenantal theology and the profound impact of his participation in the Christian–Jewish dialogue movement, by the 1980s, he would outline his thinking in a number of publications. In 1986, he published an essay entitled "Towards a Principled Pluralism" in which he presented four "Models of Pluralism" with each one offering a different rationale for his vision of improved relations between the different denominations in Jewish life.[10] In one of the models—"The Halachic Way"—Greenberg attempted to recast non-Orthodox Judaism in a halachic light, suggesting that, "It can be argued that Reform has not dropped the halacha but has given exceptional halachic weight to factors which historically were given less weight" (Greenberg, "Towards a Principled Pluralism," 30). In effect, Greenberg attempted to place non-halachic denominations on a halachic continuum by placing them in conversation with the system of Jewish law, albeit with different emphases and orienting values than their Conservative and Orthodox counterparts. Recognizing the challenge this presented, Greenberg admitted that, "To make this concept of halachic continuum credible, Reform and Reconstructionists will have to rethink their self-images" (Greenberg, "Towards a Principled Pluralism," 31). By calling on the non-halachic movements to imagine themselves as something they were not, "The Halachic Way" was an untenable argument for pluralism.

A second model—"There Is No Willful Heresy Today"—drew on the halachic ruling of the Hazon Ish,[11] which stated that "in this

---

10  To allow for smoother analysis, I consider the four models here in a different order to that which they are presented in the essay. In the original, they are presented in this order: (1) Covenant of Fate/Covenant of Destiny, (2) The Maturation of the Covenant, (3) The Halachic Way, and (4) There Is No Willful Heresy Today.

11  Rabbi Avraham Yeshayahu Karelitz (1878–1953) anonymously published a work of Jewish law entitled *Hazon Ish* (1911), which became the moniker by which he was most commonly known.

era there are no *apikorsim* and the ancient laws vis-à-vis heretics do not apply" (Greenberg, "Towards a Principled Pluralism," 31). Here, Greenberg acknowledged that, in the modern world, traditional religious assumptions are less obvious than they once may have been and that, rather than dismissing nonobservant Jews as heretics, "it is up to us to bring them back with bonds of love" (Greenberg, "Towards a Principled Pluralism," 31). This model's call to "bring them back" is reminiscent of Greenberg's condescending tone in the pages of the *Yavneh* essay.[12] As a result, it also failed to offer a defense of pluralism with which non-Orthodox Jews could readily identify.

A third model, entitled "Covenant of Fate/Covenant of Destiny," drew on the writings of Joseph B. Soloveitchik.[13] According to Greenberg, the covenant of fate was exemplified in the horrors of the Holocaust. He declared that "In the Holocaust, all Jews learned that their fate was one" (Greenberg, "Towards a Principled Pluralism," 27). Elsewhere, Greenberg has written that "There were no distinctions in the gas chambers" (Greenberg, "Will There Be One Jewish People," 6). Although the Holocaust was not the only occasion for the realization of the covenant of fate, it stood as the most poignant example of the manner in which all Jews were connected, regardless of their particular expression of Judaism.

In contrast to the involuntary nature of the covenant of fate, "The covenant of destiny reflects chosen, voluntary existence for the purpose of the realization of Jewish values and Jewish purpose in history" (Greenberg, "Towards a Principled Pluralism," 27). For Greenberg, the dialectic of these two covenants meant that Jews were bonded by the covenant of fate, yet free to diverge as a result of the covenant of destiny. He distilled it in this way: "... one must learn to distinguish validity and legitimacy. Legitimacy is derived from and applies to all groups that share the covenenat of fate. Once having

---

12  See pp. 68-75.

13  Greenberg was referencing the book that was based on an address that Soloveitchik gave at Yeshiva University in 1956. See Joseph B. Soloveitchik, *Fate and Destiny: From the Holocaust to the State of Israel* (Hoboken: Ktav, 2000).

extended that legitmacy, one has every right to criticize and disagree with the validity of actions by groups that 'violate' the covenant of destiny" (Greenberg, "Towards a Principled Pluralism," 28). However, despite the tragic fact that all may have been equal in the gas chambers, it is also the case that, in less extreme conditions, many Jews simply do not consider themselves to be part of the same covenantal community as other self-identified Jews. Put differently, this model may only work *in extremis*.

It was in the fourth model that Greenberg presented both a more ambitious understanding of his particular brand of pluralism and one that was less parochial in its orientation. Entitled "Maturation of the Covenant," Greenberg introduced this model with the assumption that "the concept of the covenant is essentially pedagogical" (Greenberg, "Towards a Principled Pluralism," 29). According to Greenberg, the covenant was purposefully structured by God so that there would be "a fundamental role for human agency in achieving the goals of the covenant" and that "over the history of the covenant, humans have been called to take on greater and greater responsibilities" (Greenberg, "Towards a Principled Pluralism," 29).[14] Simply put, Greenberg's conception of the covenant is that it is the method by which God partners with humanity in the achievement of redemption, or *Tikkun Olam*—repairing the world.[15]

---

14 Greenberg's emphasis on covenant places his work in a long tradition of Jewish covenantal thought that began with the Hebrew Bible and has continued in rabbinic and theological literature throughout Jewish history. The biblical origins of the Jewish idea of covenant (*brit*) can be found in the covenants (pl. *britot*) between God and various biblical characters, including Noah, Abraham, and Joshua, and, most significant of all, at the theophany at Sinai. The Talmud offers its own covenantal theology that includes multiple and sometimes contradictory conceptions of the covenant between God and the Jewish people. In the modern period, thinkers such as David Hartman and Eugene Borowitz—and, of course, Irving Greenberg—have taken up the mantle of covenantal thought. For a useful overview of classical and more modern manifestations of covenantal thought, see Simon Cooper, *Contemporary Covenantal Thought: Interpretations of Covenant in the Thought of David Hartman and Eugene Borowitz* (Boston: Academic Studies Press, 2012).

15 According to Greenberg, redemption means "a world filled with life, especially life in its highest, most developed form—humanity—with conditions that completely sustain the fullest dignities of all life" (Greenberg, *For the Sake of Heaven and Earth*, 52). For more on the "dignities of all life," see Chapter 9.

Greenberg's conception of the maturation of the covenant had already received its fullest treatment in his 1981 essay, "The Third Great Cycle of Jewish History." Unpacking the connection between history and theology, he presented an unfolding covenantal myth-history[16] that provided the basis for his commitment to pluralism. As the first of three covenantal stages, the biblical era was one in which God's role was dominant and humans were largely passive. Greenberg described it in this way: "During the Biblical era, the covenantal relationship itself was marked by a high degree of divine intervention ... it is very clear that God is the initiator, the senior partner, who punishes, rewards and enforces the partnership if the Jews slacken" (Greenberg, "The Third Great Cycle," 3–4). Analyzing Greenberg's system, Michael Oppenheim has added that, "In the biblical period God was perceived as the sole redeemer and the covenant was a contract between unequals. God was the adult, the actor in history, and the Jewish people, his children, remained loyal to the covenant primarily by being obedient" (Oppenheim, "Irving Greenberg," 195). In this stage of Jewish myth-history, Greenberg likened the Jewish people to children who are wholly dependent on their parents.

Contrasting the biblical era with the period of Rabbinic Judaism, Greenberg perceived the development of a greater level of partnership between God and the Jewish people. He illustrated the difference in this way:

> In the Biblical period, God's presence was manifest by splitting the sea and drowning the Egyptians. In the Second Temple siege, God did not show up ... to save the day. God had, as it were, withdrawn, become more hidden, so as to

---

16 I refer to Greenberg's covenantal theology as myth-history for two reasons: first, because it narrates a version of Jewish history that is periodized into three broad stages that are less than historically rigorous, and second, because it references mythical biblical events in the same narrative sweep as verifiable historical events such as the Holocaust and the establishment of the State of Israel. None of this undermines Greenberg's schema as a theological system; it would simply be inaccurate to describe it as purely "historical."

give humans more freedom and to call the Jews to more responsible partnership in the covenant. (Greenberg, "The Third Great Cycle," 5)

According to Greenberg, the destruction of the Second Temple in Jerusalem marked the transition from the first stage of the covenant to the second. Oppenheim has described it in this way:

In response to this catastrophe, the Rabbis rethought some of the basic concepts of Judaism. They recognized that God no longer directly intervened in history, which left the stage open to human initiative and responsibility. The covenant form was reconfigured to reflect a more equal partnership. (Oppenheim, "Irving Greenberg," 195)

In the wake of the destruction of the Second Temple, Jewish life was rebuilt in the form of Rabbinic Judaism.[17] It was through these acts of human initiative, creativity, responsibility, and rebuilding that Greenberg saw the arrival of the second stage of the covenant. According to Greenberg's schema, this second stage of the covenant lasted for almost 2,000 years.

Beginning with the European Enlightenment and Emancipation, Greenberg perceived that the modern period and, in turn, the third stage of the unfolding of the covenant, was underway. At this stage in his thinking, Greenberg claimed that it ultimately took another catastrophe—the Holocaust—to usher in the third era in earnest.[18] As Oppenheim has described it,

---

17 Of course, the late Second Temple and early rabbinic periods were much more complex than this. The simplicity of Greenberg's system only underlines its function as myth-history. For a valuable introduction to this period, see Shaye Cohen, *From the Maccabees to the Mishnah*, 2nd ed. (Louisville: Westminster John Knox Press, 2006).

18 Greenberg addressed his concern that his readers might conclude that the Holocaust was a necessary stage in the unfolding of the covenant by clarifying that "the voluntary stage is implicit in the covenantal model from the very beginning" (Greenberg, "Voluntary Covenant," 37). Years later, he would add that "the covenant model always pointed toward the idea that humanity would one day mature into full responsibility" (Greenberg, *For the Sake of Heaven and Earth*, 29). Greenberg's

> ... the Holocaust demarcates the end of the rabbinic
> paradigm and the beginning of a new stage ... History and
> the movement toward redemption is now given over to human
> efforts to an even greater extent. Correspondingly, the Jewish
> people have become the 'senior partner' in the covenantal
> enterprise. In Greenberg's words; 'God now acts primarily, at
> least on the visible level, through human activity—as is
> appropriate in a partnership whose human participant is
> growing up.' (Oppenheim, "Irving Greenberg," 195)

In this third and final stage, "the implications of the covenant are
being realized in the fullness of human responsibility" (Greenberg,
"Towards a Principled Pluralism," 29). The result is that "No longer
intimidated by instant punishment or controlled by overt rewards,
human beings are free to act out of love and internalized vision ... "
(Greenberg, "Towards a Principled Pluralism," 30). This final stage
represents the culmination of Greenberg's tri-stage covenantal theology.

The third stage of the covenant brings us back to the influence
of the Christian–Jewish dialogue and the impact of Roy Eckardt. The
defining characteristic of the third stage is the central conceptual
innovation of Greenberg's covenantal theology: the voluntary covenant. In "The Third Great Cycle," Greenberg wrote that there had
been a "reformulation of the covenant into a voluntary covenant"
and that, in light of the horrors of the Holocaust, "There can hardly be
any punishment, divine or human, that can force Jews into the
covenantal role when it is obviously far more risky to choose to be
Jewish" (Greenberg, "The Third Great Cycle," 18). In this declaration,
Greenberg unveiled his most far-reaching theological innovation.

In 1982, Greenberg published the essay, "Voluntary Covenant,"
and explicated his innovative covenantal theology in greater detail.
In a key section, subtitled "The Shattering of the Covenant," Greenberg
addressed the theological implications of the destruction of Jewish

---

important clarification resulted in modernity ultimately displacing the Holocaust as
the starting point of the third era and helped him avoid turning "the *Shoah* into the
God of the system" (Greenberg, *For the Sake of Heaven and Earth*, 29).

life during the Holocaust. Echoing Roy Eckardt, Greenberg posited that, as a result of the Holocaust, "The crisis of the covenant runs deep; one must consider the possibility that it is over." Greenberg continued:

> morally speaking, God must repent of the covenant, i.e. do *teshuvah* [repent] for having given his chosen people a task[19] that was unbearably cruel and dangerous without having provided for their protection. Morally speaking, then, God can have no claims on the Jews by dint of the covenant ... It can no longer be commanded ... If the Jews keep the covenant after the Holocaust, then it can no longer be for the reason that it is commanded or because it is enforced by reward or punishment. (Greenberg, "Voluntary Covenant," 34–35)

Stopping short of Eckardt's claim that the covenant had ended, Greenberg concluded: "What then happened to the covenant? I submit that its authority was broken" (Greenberg, "Voluntary Covenant," 35). The significance of this claim cannot be overstated. Greenberg's suggestion that the obligatory nature of the covenant between God and the Jewish people had ended represented a clean break with Jewish tradition.

The implications of the voluntary stage of the covenant were central to Greenberg's emerging theology of intra-Jewish pluralism. Describing the meaning of this theological innovation for Jewish life, Steven T. Katz has pointed out that

> in an age of voluntarism rather than coercion, living Jewishly under the covenant can no longer be interpreted monolithically, that is, only in a strict halakhic fashion. A genuine Jewish pluralism, a Judaism of differing options and interpretations, is the only legitimate foundation in the age of Auschwitz. Orthodox observance, no less than

---

19  That is, the task of upholding the covenant.

> Reform, Conservative, or 'secular' practices are voluntary—none can claim either automatic authority or exclusive priority in the contemporary Jewish world. (Katz, "Irving (Yitzchak) Greenberg," 71)

In Greenberg's own words:

> In the age of the voluntary covenant ... all who opt to live as Jews automatically state their readiness for martyrdom, not only for themselves but for their children and grand-children as well ... In the new era, the voluntary covenant is the theological base of a genuine pluralism. Pluralism is not a matter of tolerance made necessary by living in a non-Jewish reality, nor is it pity for one who does not know any better. It is a recognition that all Jews have chosen to make the fundamental Jewish statement at great personal risk and cost. The present denominations are paths for the covenant-minded all leading toward the final goal. (Greenberg, "Voluntary Covenant," 38)

Greenberg's innovative contribution to post-Holocaust covenantal theology provided a basis for his claim that all expressions of Judaism and Jewish life were equally valid. As he wrote in his first reference to the voluntary stage of the covenant, "Pluralism is also the theological consequence of the reformulation of the covenant into a voluntary covenant ... Given the voluntary nature of Jewish commitment, there cannot be one imposed standard of Jewish loyalty or excellence" (Greenberg, "The Third Great Cycle," 18). In the new era, Greenberg suggested, "A fuller covenantal role, properly understood, implies that God must allow human responsibility to be exercised responsibly ... Under this approach, all movements have in common covenantal motivation and commitment" (Greenberg, "Towards a Principled Pluralism," 29). In short, for

Greenberg, the maturation of the covenant implied an inherent justification for recognizing the validity of the widest range of expressions of Judaism. This conclusion, arrived at through sustained and transformative encounters with Christian theologians, would become a central pillar of Greenberg's theology of hybrid Judaism.

# Chapter 7

# Klal Yisrael

In addition to influencing the development of his own covenantal theology, Greenberg's involvement in the Christian–Jewish dialogue movement also provided a model for his vision for improved intra-Jewish relations. In the 1980s, he wrote that if relations between Jewish groups were going to improve, dialogue would need to take place on "a popular level, modeled on the 'living room dialogue' of the Jewish–Christian experience" (Greenberg, "Will There Be One Jewish People," 7). On more than one occasion he lamented the fact that "the Jewish community developed three organizations to insure continual dialogue with Christians[1] while it has only the Synagogue Council [of America] for intra-Jewish religious contact" (Greenberg, "End of Emancipation" 62). For Greenberg, the need for a more effective approach was undeniable. Writing in the pages of the journal *Conservative Judaism*—itself an example of the kind of cross-denominational discourse he was calling for—he declared in his essay, "The End of Emancipation" (1976), that

> The community needs many places where rabbis and scholars
> can come together in serious fashion. Every time there is a
> crunch on religious or halakhic matters, the participants line
> up along denominational lines because there has been no

---

1 Greenberg did not list the names of the organizations. Two of the organizations he was likely referring to were the National Council of Christians and Jews (NCCJ) and the National Interreligious Affairs Department of the American Jewish Committee.

serious bridge-building or alliances between the groups … the lack of mechanism for dialogue becomes a major obstacle to the movement and constitutes a spiritual and moral threat to the renewal of Judaism.

His sense of foreboding led him to advance a radical idea:

One might propose that nobody should be allowed to practice in the rabbinate after leaving The Jewish Theological Seminary or Hebrew Union College or Yeshiva University, unless they first study together in a center that crosses party lines … Here and in a host of areas where the tradition needs reform, the sociological question of contact is as crucial as the intellectual, philosophical question of what is possible. (Greenberg, "End of Emancipation," 62)

To date, no American rabbinical school program includes such a requirement. Nevertheless, Greenberg's emphasis on the importance of "contact" (read: encounter) between rabbis from the different denominational streams of Judaism was significant and would become the basis for influential programs he would later establish at CLAL.[2] His identification of the relationship between "contact" and "reform" was especially important. It represented his acknowledgment that encounters between members of different denominations in the Jewish community would result in transformative change. His call for dialogue was rooted in the commitment that "Through such dialogues, people overcome stereotypes. They learn there is real commitment in the other groups to values which they also respect and desire" (Greenberg, "Will There Be One Jewish People," 7). Although not yet postethnic, Greenberg was already able to recognize the transformative impact of encounter.

---

2  David Hartman would also go on to establish successful programs at the Shalom Hartman Institute, in Israel, geared toward rabbis from different denominations coming together to study.

Although Greenberg was heavily influenced by the Christian–Jewish dialogue movement, he also understood the transformative power of cross-group encounters from personal experiences within the Jewish community. Beginning in the summer of 1965, Greenberg participated in an intra-Jewish dialogue group that was as influential as his experiences with the Christian–Jewish dialogue movement. As Greenberg recalled, "By 1965, [Rabbi] David Hartman persuaded a wealthy lay leader to underwrite a week of learning together for a group of scholars. We invited the best Orthodox thinkers we knew and—there being some money left over—invited some Conservative and Reform thinkers as well" (Butler and Nagel, *My Yeshiva College*, 183). In doing so, Hartman and Greenberg ignored the denominational divisions that so often separated American Jewish leaders from one another. Elie Wiesel recalled the 1965 gathering, writing that "Rabbi David Hartman ... organize[d] a 'pluralistic' Jewish conference ... There were about thirty of us there: Orthodox, Conservative and Reform rabbis and others ... " (Portnoff, Diamond, and Yaffe, *Emil L. Fackenheim*, xi). These were groundbreaking events bringing together individuals who would become major leaders in the American Jewish community and beyond for the next half century. Precious little has been written about them and, as Wiesel recalled, there were "no papers or lectures ... Only debates on the situation of the Jewish people" (Portnoff, Diamond, and Yaffe, *Emil L. Fackenheim*, xi).[3] Nevertheless, these encounters were of great significance for Greenberg and they exposed him, in a deeply personal way, to thinkers outside of the Orthodox camp.

---

3  Greenberg had a different recollection when he wrote that, "At the group's first meeting in 1965, I read a first paper on the implications of the Holocaust for Judaism entitled, 'God's Acts in History'" (Greenberg, *For the Sake of Heaven and Earth*, 11). It appears that this paper had a significant impact on the Reform rabbi and philosopher, Emil Fackenheim (1916–2003), who was also present. In the preface to his great work of Holocaust theology, *God's Presence in History: Jewish Affirmations and Philosophical Reflections* (1970), Fackenheim wrote, "I owe a fundamental debt to Irving Greenberg's concept of 'orienting experience': his stubbornly historical thinking has liberated me from some false philosophical abstractions" (Fackenheim, *God's Presence in History*, v).

Throughout the rest of the 1960s, Greenberg participated in a number of gatherings that would expose him up close to non-Orthodox Jews. In 1966, he was invited to present a paper at the annual meeting of the Board of Editors of the respected journal of Jewish thought, *Judaism*. His paper was part of a larger symposium that addressed the question, "Jewish Religious Unity: Is It Possible?" Inspired by Hartman's Canadian gathering the year before, the symposium included a diverse array of participants. Greenberg's very presence alongside the founder of the Reconstructionist movement, Mordecai M. Kaplan, Reform theologian, Jakob J. Petuchowski, and Conservative scholar, Seymour Siegel, demonstrated his commitment to intra-group relations.

So exceptional were these cross-denominational gatherings that, on three different occasions toward the end of the 1960s, *The New York Times* reported on them. In the first article, published in May 1967 under the headline "Rethinking by Jews," Greenberg was described as part of an "ecumenical 'underground' [that] has developed in recent years consisting of younger rabbis and theologians from all three branches" (Fiske, "Rethinking by Jews," E4). A second article about the gatherings in Canada was published in 1969 under the heading "3 Branches Meet in Effort to Improve Ties." In another article from 1969, the newspaper reported that: "Jewish Theologians Are Reviving an Increase in the Recovery of Traditional Customs and Teachings." Again, Greenberg was cited alongside a list of notable Jewish thinkers.[4] Clearly, Greenberg was spending a great deal of time during the 1960s in up close and personal encounters with Jews from across the denominational and theological spectrum. Forty years later, Greenberg reminisced about the Canadian gatherings and acknowledged the personal transformation that had taken place, writing that, " ... I was orienting myself to a *Klal Yisrael*[5]

---

4   Other participants in these various gatherings included Eliezer Berkovits, Eugene B. Borowitz, Emil Fackenheim, Maurice Friedman, Inge Lederer Gibel, Arthur Green, Abraham Joshua Heschel, Aharon Lichtenstein, Hershel Matt, Emanuel Rackman, Alvin J. Reines, Fritz Rothschild, Richard L. Rubenstein, Herman Schaalman, Steven S. Schwarzschild, Jacob Taubes, J. E. Ittamar Wohlgelernter, Arnold J. Wolf, Michael Wyschogrod, and Walter S. Wurzburger.

5   *Klal Yisrael* might be best translated as Jewish Peoplehood, suggesting that all members of the Jewish community are connected to each other in some tribal

community of Orthodox-Conservative-Reform rabbis ... " (Butler and Nagel, *My Yeshiva College*, 184). Greenberg was part of a fledgling cross-denominational Jewish community, even as he was part of its creation.

Within a year of the first of the Canadian gatherings, an interview with Greenberg was published in the April 28, 1966, edition of the Yeshiva University student newspaper, *The Commentator*, under the title "Dr. Greenberg Discusses Orthodoxy, YU, Viet Nam, & Sex." By this time, Greenberg had become a well-established and highly popular instructor at YU; the publication of the interview stands as a watershed moment for Greenberg's career. The interview would put him on the map as one of the most progressive thinkers in the American Orthodox Jewish community. As the title of the interview suggests, Greenberg discussed a number of hot-button issues, especially for an Orthodox rabbi and member of the faculty of the history department at Yeshiva University. Greenberg called on his readers to "not necessarily accept all of America, but at least we should explore its attitudes and integrate those that illuminate and deepen our traditional Jewish framework" (Goldberg, "Dr. Greenberg," 6). He also called on Orthodoxy to "train a body of scholars in the new fields of study, especially in Biblical criticism," to embark on a "thorough re-examination of the *Shulchan Orach*,"[6] and declared the need to develop "new *halachot* about sex" (Goldberg, "Dr. Greenberg," 10). Addressing any one of these topics would have made Greenberg stand out; addressed together in one interview reflected just how far his thinking had advanced.

Responding to the question "What do you believe is the essential element in Jewish theology?," Greenberg answered, "The covenant idea, the belief that an infinite G-d is concerned for man and will enter into a personal relationship with him ... Ideally, the Jew

---

fashion. For a valuable analysis of the notion of Jewish Peoplehood, see Noam Pianko, *Jewish Peoplehood: An American Innovation* (New Brunswick: Rutgers University Press, 2015).

6  Literally, "The prepared table." This is the name of the sixteenth-century work of Jewish law, authored by Joseph ben Ephraim Karo (1488–1575).

performs this function by accepting the covenants of Abraham and Moses—by fulfilling their *halachic* obligations to man and G-d" (Goldberg, "Dr. Greenberg," 6). This response could have been uttered by any traditional Orthodox Jew; however, in a creative reinterpretation of the traditional covenantal idea that each Jew is obligated to abide by Jewish law (*halachah*), Greenberg asserted his new "Klal Yisrael" identity and added that, "I believe that the definition of a Jew is one who takes the covenant idea seriously, who struggles to find its vitality in his own life. It doesn't matter to me whether one calls himself Reform, Conservative or Orthodox" (Goldberg, "Dr. Greenberg," 6). In his answer to the very first question of the interview, Greenberg immediately broached the subject of how Orthodox Jews should relate to members of the other denominations in the American Jewish community. His disregard for denominational labels and his expansive understanding of the covenant reflected the influence of the Canadian gatherings and a deeper interest in the religious lives of individual Jews rather than their particular affiliations.

When the interviewer followed up with the question, "Do you feel the categories 'Reform,' 'Conservative,' and 'Orthodox' have any meaning?," Greenberg further clarified his position:

> The main reality in these categories is an institutional one. But too often the three classifications only blind one's vision. Today Judaism intellectually is shattered in a thousand different directions, and when we admit this, we'll be able to begin struggling with the real problems facing the American Jewish community. These classifications make it seem that any problem which arises can be neatly fit into three boxes, each one representing a denominational view. But this is just not true. (Goldberg, "Dr. Greenberg," 6)

Greenberg's suggestion was that there was a need for more nuanced ways of thinking about the American Jewish community that would go beyond the familiar tripartite denominational division. It is noteworthy that Greenberg did not mention the Holocaust explicitly at any point in the lengthy interview. Instead of the Holocaust, Greenberg turned to modernity as the catalyst for rethinking intra-group relations. When asked, "What is the primary problem facing today's Orthodox community?," Greenberg responded that

> Orthodoxy refuses to come out of the East European ghetto psychologically ... Orthodoxy refuses to show sympathy to those who respond authentically to the fact that Orthodoxy has lost all connection with modern life. Conservative and Reform have taken the risk and dealt seriously with the problem of Judaism's relevancy to modern life. (Goldberg, "Dr. Greenberg," 6)

In this response, Greenberg lauded the willingness of Conservative and Reform Judaism to respond to the challenges posed by the modern world, while Orthodoxy refused to do the same. As David Singer has observed in his analysis of the *Commentator* interview, "Greenberg's slaps at Orthodoxy were matched by praise directed at Conservative and Reform Judaism" (Singer, "Debating Modern Orthodoxy," 117).

At the same time, Greenberg did offer a critique of Conservative and Reform Judaism, stating that, even as they confronted the challenge of modernity, " ... they came up with the wrong answers." According to Greenberg, "Too many time [*sic*] the Conservative movement changes *halachah* because popular opinion demands the change. I believe that changes in *halachah* should not be the result of popular opinion, but the result of deliberate consideration by the *gedolim*"[7] (Goldberg, "Dr. Greenberg," 6). Although he did not specify, his critique was most likely in reference to decisions such as the controversial 1950 ruling of the Conservative Movement's Law Committee of the Rabbinical Assembly, which permitted driving to

---

7 Literally, "The Great Ones." This was an uncharacteristic affirmation of the prevalent Orthodox view that only certain rabbis, as a result of their stature in the community, can effect changes in Jewish law.

synagogue on the Sabbath. Nevertheless, even as he disagreed with aspects of Conservative and Reform Judaism, Greenberg honored and valued what he saw as their responsiveness to modern life. While the interview did not begin to describe a systematic theology of religious pluralism, it did provide some indication of Greenberg's early thinking about and appreciation for non-Orthodox denominations of Judaism.

There was a strong backlash at Yeshiva University immediately after the interview was published. According to one report, "The ink had barely dried on Greenberg's interview when a furious reaction set in" (Singer, "Debating Modern Orthodoxy," 117). Greenberg responded in writing in the May 12th edition of *The Commentator*, under the headlines "Greenberg Clarifies and Defends his Views," "Student Criticism Spurs Dr. Greenberg's Answer," and "Professor's Comments Prompt Torrent of Protest." In his response, Greenberg restated his major positions from the original interview, albeit in softer terms. Both the original interview and Greenberg's subsequent clarification elicited a harsh critique from his colleague and fellow Yeshiva University faculty member, Aharon Lichtenstein, in the June 2nd edition.

Like Greenberg, Lichtenstein was born in 1933, was a student of Joseph B. Soloveitchik,[8] and would go on to receive his doctorate from Harvard. After completing his Ph.D. in English Literature, Lichtenstein "taught [English] for several years at Stern College, Yeshiva's women's division, before moving on to a position as a star Talmudist at Yeshiva's rabbinic seminary" (Singer, "Debating Modern Orthodoxy," 114). Lichtenstein's sharp response to Greenberg "made no secret of his belief that Greenberg's slashing attack on contemporary Orthodoxy was a calculated move intended to provoke controversy at Yeshiva and thus force a confrontation with Greenberg's religious views" (Singer, "Debating Modern Orthodoxy," 115).

---

8   Greenberg came under the influence of Soloveitchik in the 1950s during his tenure as the rabbi of the Young Israel of Brookline. Lichtenstein became a student of Soloveitchik during his undergraduate years and while studying for rabbinic ordination at Yeshiva University. He would eventually become Soloveitchik's son-in-law.

As David Singer has noted, "Lichtenstein came down hard on Greenberg," criticizing both the content of his ideas and the manner in which they were articulated (Singer, "Debating Modern Orthodoxy," 118). Expressing his concern regarding "the fundamental posture implicitly assumed throughout the article," Lichtenstein suggested that "there are matters about which you and I have no business issuing manifestos altogether" (Lichtenstein, "Rav Lichtenstein," 7). Focusing on Greenberg's vision of the relationship between the Jewish community and the open society, Lichtenstein demurred, writing that "I do not think that we should immerse ourselves in American society to the extent that you seem to advocate" (Lichtenstein, "Rav Lichtenstein," 8). His commitment to "an axiological hierarchy" (Lichtenstein, "Rav Lichtenstein," 8) that prioritized the needs of the Jewish community over that of others led Lichtenstein to reject Greenberg's overtures to the open society. David Singer has aptly summarized the difference between Greenberg and Lichtenstein in this way: "A key marker of Lichtenstein's centrism was his willingness to set limits to cultural openness, something that Greenberg refused to do" (Singer, "Debating Modern Orthodoxy," 124). Like the critics of Greenberg's engagement with the Christian–Jewish dialogue movement,[9] Lichtenstein echoed Horace Kallen's desire for cultural separation, while Greenberg was already attracted, although still with reservations, to the possibilites of encounter. We will return to Greenberg's thinking about the open society in greater detail in the next chapter.

Lichtenstein also expressed concerns for the survival of Orthodoxy, writing that "Our primary goal must be the more selfish—yes selfish—one of surviving as a viable tradition ..." (Lichtenstein, "Rav Lichtenstein," 8). Given his concerns about Orthodoxy, Lichtenstein made it clear that, with regard to intra-Jewish relations, "I ... disagree with your tactical approach towards Conservative and Reform Judaism" (Lichtenstein, "Rav Lichtenstein," 8). For Lichtenstein, to downplay the very real differences between Orthodoxy and the

---

9  See pp. 80-83.

progressive denominations with regard to their characterization of "the Torah as God's revealed word and of the tradition derived therefrom" would, in his words, undermine "our efforts to maintain the integrity of Torah and *Halacha*" (Lichtenstein, "Rav Lichtenstein," 8). Given his concerns, it should come as no surprise that Greenberg's ideas regarding biblical criticism, the re-examination of Jewish law, the covenantal relationship of Orthodox and non-Orthodox Jews, and the extent to which Orthodoxy was out of touch with the modern world, all came under fire from Lichtenstein.

According to Greenberg, the entire episode was somewhat of a shock to him. Almost 40 years after the original interview, Greenberg recalled that "I sat in my office for hours talking with a student about my thinking on Modern Orthodoxy. I spoke unguardedly … The student never told me that he was writing up the conversation with intent to publish"[10] (Butler and Nagel, *My Yeshiva College*, 84). Recalling his lengthy clarification to the editor, Greenberg later acknowledged that, "I believed in what I said, but the printed words went considerably beyond what many people were prepared to hear. In my written response to the furor, I disingenuously tried to soften and minimize the implications of my words—which convinced no one" (Butler and Nagel, *My Yeshiva College*, 184). As we have already seen,[11] this would not be the first time that Greenberg attempted to cloak the full meaning of his ideas. However, his public spat with Lichtenstein did mean that Greenberg would have his first experience as a controversial public figure within American Orthodox Judaism. Ultimately, his commitment to *Klal Yisrael* would mean that he would never regain his footing in the mainstream Orthodox community.

---

10  The student was Harold (Hillel) Goldberg. Greenberg's retrospective claim itself became the subject of public debate in the pages of *The Commentator*. See "Letters," *The Commentator*, May 17, 2005.

11  See pp. 81-82.

# Chapter 8

# The Open Society

Inherent in Greenberg's commitment to improved intra-Jewish relations and his involvement in the Christian–Jewish dialogue movement is an affirmation of the importance of encounter. During the 1960s, Greenberg began to explore the meaning of encounter—framed in the language of "the open society"—in two important scholarly publications. In 1965, he published his first academic paper in a scholarly journal and shared his initial fears about encounter. The paper, entitled "Adventure in Freedom—Or Escape from Freedom?," was printed in the pages of the *American Jewish Historical Quarterly* and claimed that, even though the *Jews* had apparently "made it" in America, it appeared that their *Judaism* had not been quite as fortunate. At the outset, Greenberg observed that "The occupational and income distribution of Jewish household heads and their median incomes are the highest of the three national religious groupings"[1] and that, in terms of schooling, "Jewish educational achievement is the highest of all religious groups collectively." Furthermore, Greenberg pointed out, "Over 87 per cent of Jews live in the urban centers which are the shapers and leaders of American culture today" (Greenberg, "Adventure in Freedom," 5–6). He went on to list the presence of Jews in the professional and academic ranks, their representation throughout the mass media empire, and the popularity of American Jewish literature. Finally, Greenberg pointed to a distinct decline in anti-Semitism. Following his laundry list of statistics that demonstrated what appeared to be the

---

1  Like Will Herberg, Greenberg referred only to Catholics, Jews, and Protestants.

resounding success of American Jews, Greenberg addressed the question of Jewish identity and group life in America.

Greenberg drew on a wide range of demographic studies and sociological works from the likes of Milton Gordon, Nathan Glazer, and Marshall Sklare to inform his understanding of the American Jewish situation. Describing the now familiar demise of the consensus narrative,[2] Greenberg pointed to "the shattering of the traditional American self-image—the unself-conscious white Anglo-Saxon Protestant cultural image which had dominated American life, public school education and culture" (Greenberg, "Adventure in Freedom," 8–9). According to Greenberg, the historical movement was that,

> Up until the late nineteenth century, the bulk of immigrants were assimilated to this ethos with no serious modifications of the image. Now, in the widely disseminated formulation of Will Herberg, the picture was restructured to that of a tri-faith culture, Protestant, Catholic and Jew. (Greenberg, "Adventure in Freedom," 9)

In this excerpt, Greenberg charted the movement from Anglo-conformism to tri-faith America.[3] In doing so, he also located his own consideration of the changing nature of American Jewish identity in the context of the century-long arc of sociological theories of group life outlined in Part I.

Given these changes, Greenberg suggested that, despite all appearances, the results would not be positive for American Jewry. In his words:

> … as far as the Jews are concerned, we are not 'beyond the melting pot.'[4] The organic identity which the Jews in Eastern

---

2 See pp. 21-22.

3 This phrase comes from Kevin M. Schultz's *Tri-Faith America: How Catholics and Jews Held Postwar America to Its Protestant Promise* (New York: Oxford University Press, 2011).

4 Greenberg was almost certainly referencing Glazer and Moynihan's work of the same title, published two years earlier.

Europe tended to take for granted has been shattered. And for American Jews, the essential element which makes possible the life and continuity of a group—an integrated identity, a distinctive self image of the individual and the group—has been seriously weakened. It is true that a group identity of sorts has persisted but the life style of the American Jew indicates that he is a quintessential middle class American secularist in faith, culture, and practice. (Greenberg, "Adventure in Freedom," 10–11)

Here, Greenberg expressed his fear that the triple melting pot had undermined the future of the American Jewish community, ultimately transforming American Jews into so many "middle class Americans." However, even as Greenberg's words were reminiscent of Kallen's call for the maintenance of distinct group identities, he then proceeded to criticize the "pluralistic ideological liberalism of intellectuals" that "evokes mellow images of variety, respect for differences, and nonconformity." Ultimately, according to Greenberg, "the pluralists' self-congratulation is as premature as the Jewish community's 'success' ethos" (Greenberg, "Adventure in Freedom," 10).

At this early stage in his thinking, the source of Greenberg's concerns was the problem of encounter. Greenberg perceived the social mixing that was becoming more prevalent in American society as the cause of the "shattering" and "weakening" of American Jewish identity:

The decline in anti-Semitism and increasing acceptance of Jews reduces the ethnic closed environment. Isolation is fast shrinking as constantly increasing forms of communication, values indoctrination and personal contact grow. There is simply no place to hide to preserve ethnic or other commit-ments from outside contact. Passive identification falls easy victim of the mere encounter with the majority culture which is, after all, different or it yields to the dynamic in various forms of modern culture. As Walter J. Ong puts it, "The medieval types and other primitive types of coexistence by isolation, with their consequent pluralisms based on geographical divisions, are no longer acceptable ... The very lack of effective communication which lent plausibility to isolationism was a temporary condition, destined to be liquidated ... " (Greenberg, "Adventure in Freedom," 14)

Greenberg understood that the open society meant that encounters between Jews and those identified with other ethnic, cultural, and religious groups were increasing in both number and intensity, thus presenting a threat to Jewish identity and affirmation. One can even detect a lamenting tone in his observation that there was a "decline in anti-Semitism and increasing acceptance of Jews," resulting in a situation in which it was harder for American Jews to remain ethnically isolated. Greenberg was unequivocal in his concern that "isolation is fast shrinking," that there are "increasing forms of communications," and that there is "simply no place to hide." Turning to Walter J. Ong, Greenberg found support in his suggestion that a brand of pluralism that is predicated on ethnic separation—for example, Horace Kallen's cultural pluralism—was no longer viable in contemporary American society. Essentially, Greenberg perceived the increase in encounters between individuals and across social groups as a serious and inevitable threat to American Jewish identity.[5]

Greenberg went on to suggest that the college campus was the setting in which the threat of contact was greatest. He pointed out that "College ... is increasingly the major area of socialization and marriage ... The college setting is highly destructive of vestigial Jewish loyalties [where] proximity to non-Jews is highest" and that "All this takes on stark significance when one considers that 80 per cent of eligible Jews go to college and the rate is rising" (Greenberg, "Adventure in Freedom," 14–16). Greenberg identified the college experience as presenting a significant existential threat to the Jewish community. As he put it bluntly, "In this case the vulnerability is

---

5   In a discussion of Greenberg's essay published in the same edition of the journal, Marshall Sklare described Greenberg as "depressed and depressing." See Marshall Sklare, "Discussant." *American Jewish Historical Quarterly* 55, no. 1 (1965): 32-36.

heightened by contact with the active proselytizing faiths with a mission which dominate[s] such groups. I refer, of course, to the religion of the Enlightenment, Americanized ..." (Greenberg, "Adventure in Freedom," 16). Greenberg's suspicions regarding the "Americanization" that was taking place on college campuses was rooted in what he described as "the naturalism whose faith is in the rational order of efficient causation; whose method is science, whose morality is humanism and whose messianic hope is the redemption of mankind through man's self-understanding and rationality" (Greenberg, "Adventure in Freedom," 16). In effect, Greenberg thought of the American college campus as the continuation of the European Enlightenment, with all that it entailed for Jewish life.[6] For him, the sum of these forces could lead to only one conclusion: "To put it in a nutshell: third generation status, rising wealth, higher education, suburban residence, academic-governmental-intellectual occupations, more social contact with non-Jews, all correlate positively with a higher intermarriage rate" (Greenberg, "Adventure in Freedom," 18) and, in effect, departure from the Jewish community.[7] For Greenberg, the open society—exemplified in its purest form on the college campus—posed a grave existential threat to Jewish life in America.

In short, Greenberg lamented the possibility that American Judaism would be the victim of American Jews' success. Greenberg's description of the direction of Jewish life in America—supported by copiously cited sociological studies—indirectly supported Milton Gordon's suggestion that Horace Kallen's conception of cultural pluralism, in which groups are free and equal, but unthreatened by contact with each other, was nothing more than wishful thinking. In Greenberg's estimation, technological advancements and geographic mobility paired with the upward mobility of American Jews created a mid-twentieth-century reality in which Jews and non-Jews

---

6  Recall that Greenberg wrote that "the Emancipation and westernization ... washed away the Torah centered community framework of our life as a people" (Greenberg, "Yavneh," 47).

7  The American Jewish community in the 1960s was much less welcoming to inter-marriage than it is today. As such, the correlation between intermarriage and estrangement from the Jewish community was assumed.

were destined to have direct encounters with each other that could only result in a weakening of Jewish identity and affirmation.

In one of the few optimistic moments in Greenberg's essay,[8] he wrote that "there are a number of Jewish groups which are seeking an integrated, mature Jewish individual and group identity" (Greenberg, "Adventure in Freedom," 19). Not surprisingly, in the footnotes, Greenberg cited the "Yavneh Movement," of which he was still a key figure, as one of a small number of examples of such Jewish groups.[9] Drawing an unexpected contrast to his suggestion that encounter represented an all-out threat to American Judaism, Greenberg encouraged these groups to find a balance and "seek to assimilate American experience and culture critically rather than merely adjusting Judaism passively as a Kultur-religion or reshaping the Jewish image in a non-Jewish world" (Greenberg, "Adventure in Freedom," 19). Reading this section in light of the rest of the essay, one is struck by the tension inherent in Greenberg's early thinking. He was both fearful of and, at the same time, open to, encounters with the open society. On the one hand, he perceived propinquity to non-Jews and intermarriage with them as the death knell of American Judaism. On the other hand, he was well aware of the growing integration of Jewish life in the broader American context, encouraging his readers to be open to the best of American society and to assimilate those aspects. Surprisingly, at no point did Greenberg call for greater separation and isolation from, or for a rejection of, the open society. Rather, Greenberg acknowledged the tension and concluded with these words:

> It remains to be seen whether the history of American Jewry will culminate in a renewal which retroactively will show its

8 Over the course of a 20-page essay, Greenberg devoted less than one page to perceived positive developments in American Jewry.

9 Greenberg also referenced the Orthodox "traditionalist groups" cited by Charles Liebman, a "new theology group" within the Reform movement and, from the Conservative movement, the Leaders Training Fellowship (LTF) of the Jewish Theological Seminary of America and the movement's Ramah summer camps. See Charles S. Liebman, "A Sociological Analysis of Contemporary Orthodoxy," *Judaism* 13, no. 3 (1964): 285–304, and Ben Hamon, "The Reform Rabbis Debate Theology," *Judaism* 12, no. 4 (1963): 479–486.

experience to have been a great adventure in freedom of the mind and heart of Jewry, or whether it will end with an escape from freedom into dissolution. (Greenberg, "Adventure in Freedom," 21)

It would take a number of years before Greenberg would fully embrace the transformative power of encounter as a force for good, not only for American Jewry, but for all of humanity. Ultimately, his theology would provide the rationale for his abiding commitment to the open society and the basis on which he could overcome his concerns regarding the apparent danger it posed for the American Jewish community.

Three years later, in 1968, Greenberg returned to the subject of the open society. In what would be his only publication in the pages of *Tradition: A Journal of Orthodox Jewish Thought*, "Jewish Values and the Changing American Ethic" would also be his most explicit treatment of pluralism in the 1960s and one that would lay the groundwork for his future explorations of the subject. Echoing ideas from "Adventure in Freedom," the essay opened with a description of the widespread success of American society, pointing to a level of affluence that "is literally unprecedented in history" (Greenberg, "Jewish Values," 42). Greenberg saw in this affluence a grave danger. Channeling his training in the *Musar* tradition, Greenberg railed against what he described as "the gradual emergence of a hedonistic affluent society" (Greenberg, "Jewish Values," 43) in which consumption and the "fun syndrome" had become the guiding values in American society. As a result, Greenberg posited that Judaism needed to respond to the materialistic tendency in the new American ethos, not by rejecting materialism out of hand, but rather by recognizing that "Holiness in mainstream Judaism involves sanctifying the secular and experiencing it in value oriented ways" (Greenberg, "Jewish Values," 54).[10] The result was an openness to the new reality that placed limits on the hedonism that had resulted from the great affluence of American society.

---

10  Greenberg would later refer to this as "Holy secularity." For more on the concept, see Irving Greenberg, "The Third Great Cycle of Jewish History." *Perspectives* 1981: 1–26.

Greenberg warned that the combination of increasingly hedonistic affluence and a rapidly changing social structure in the form of the open society held significant implications for group life in America. He described the situation in these terms:

> This new affluence has gone hand in hand with increasing concentration of population in large cities and with steady expansion of the mass media of communication and inter-class, inter-cultural exposure. Urbanization and indus-trialization alike dictate a new impersonality, emphasis on technological efficiency, sophistication and pluralism of perception, values and relationships. Universal concerns and awareness of differing cultures and value systems are constantly broadcast in every medium and individualized by people. The old provincial or particularistic cultural settings are crumbling before this communications explosion. (Greenberg, "Jewish Values," 42)

In this new "American Ethic," Greenberg perceived the collision of different people and ideas into one another, resulting in the end of provincialism and particularism. In almost prophetic terms, Greenberg articulated his understanding of the meaning of the changes that were taking place in society all around him. Striking a revolutionary note in his analysis of the changes that were afoot in the new social reality, Greenberg wrote that,

> The result is clearly the overthrow of an older ethos and the emergence of a new American (soon to be, world wide) ethic. Broadly speaking, the earlier ethic was particularistic, normative, with an ascribed identity for the individual (a product of the homogeneous and relatively isolated cultural condition) and anti-hedonist or ascetic in its flavor (a product of the scarcity and need for high productivity and investment levels of the economy). The new ethic is more universalist, relativist, self and pleasure oriented. (Greenberg, "Jewish Values," 42–43)

Here, Greenberg claimed that the very nature of identity was undergoing change in the wake of the "overthrow" of the old ethic. In his description of the changes that were afoot, he sketched the broad outlines of the shift from cultural pluralism to what would later be termed postethnicity. According to Greenberg, in the older ethic, identities were particularistic, that is, distinct from one another. Echoing Horace Kallen's statement that "Men ... cannot change their grandfathers" (Kallen, *Culture and Democracy*, 114–115), he suggested that identities were "normative" and "ascribed." By direct contrast, in the new ethic, Greenberg anticipated something akin to David Hollinger's postethnic America, in which identity is "universalist" and "relativist." In the new ethic, previously distinct and fixed identities were now available to all. Greenberg perceived in the new ethic of the American open society of the late 1960s a fundamental change in the nature of individual and group identity as a direct result of the increasing opportunities for encounters between people.

This changing social reality was not just a threat to the old American ethos in general, but also to the Jewish community in particular. Greenberg wrote: "As it stands now, Judaism is bleeding to death in America. Many of its best sons and daughters are constantly attracted to the new ethos and feel that they must abandon the old to embrace the new" (Greenberg, "Jewish Values," 50). As a result, he continued, "There are two major types of response that can be given to this crisis. One possibility is a withdrawal from the culture which is saturated with the new values to a cultural and religious island (perhaps, one should say, ghetto) within ... The other choice is to try to accept, refine and ultimately master the new environment and ethic" (Greenberg, "Jewish Values," 50). Given the choices, one would not be surprised had Greenberg called for a hasty retreat. After all, how could the American Jewish minority stand up to the tidal wave of the changing American ethic that Greenberg so powerfully described? However, Greenberg's parenthetical reference to the "ghetto" betrayed his bias that retreat represented a march backwards into a pre-Enlightenment era, when Jews were physically cut off from the general society.[11] But the second option would require work, as Greenberg pointed out, it "would require new conceptions, techniques and emphases" (Greenberg, "Jewish Values," 50). In short, for Judaism to prosper in the new American ethic, it would have to undergo significant change.

Greenberg considered both options. In the first case, it would be difficult to be "hermetically sealed off in a society such as ours. The mass media reach everywhere. Ours is a highly porous society, culturally speaking" (Greenberg, "Jewish Values," 51). Moreover, Greenberg declared that "withdrawal reflects not only simplicity of faith but perhaps also a poverty of imagination. It sees Judaism as possible only in a certain cultural setting and ethic" (Greenberg, "Jewish Values," 53). This was unacceptable to Greenberg, whose theological commitment to Judaism demanded that "If it is divine, surely it can outlast the wreckage of an earlier ethos. If the voice from Sinai crystallized for one glorious moment in Roptchitz and Berditchev, can it not crystallize again in Rockaway and Boston?" (Greenberg, "Jewish Values," 53). In other words, Judaism must be able to withstand the open society without having to retreat from it.

Instead of opting for withdrawal, Greenberg called for direct engagement with the new ethic. But what of the dangers of encounter? In response to the changing social reality in which different people would have no choice but to encounter one another, Greenberg identified two popular trends: "On the one hand, liberal universalism tends to assume the disappearance of all particular groups. Thus, in the name of freedom, the right to exist differently is challenged or undermined" (Greenberg, "Jewish Values," 55–56). Echoing Zangwill's melting pot, this approach meant that group identity would be undermined by liberal universalism. Whereas, "On the other hand, the new respect for all men and the openness and interchange lead to the possibility of true pluralism" (Greenberg, "Jewish Values," 55–56). This approach suggested that there was an

---

11 This has been attempted in a number of cases. Possibly the most far-reaching example is that of New Square in Rockland County, NY. New Square is a village inhabited almost entirely by adherents to the Skverer Hasidic sect.

opportunity to reassert identity in the open society. In this formulation, Greenberg presented an innovative understanding of pluralism that was predicated on "openness" and "interchange" instead of isolation and withdrawal. It was this second approach that Greenberg affirmed.

Here, for the first time, Greenberg employed the language of "pluralism" to refer to an affirmative model for American Jews to navigate the changing American ethic. As he put it, "true pluralism" meant "genuine acceptance of the Jew for the first time and a willingness to recognize his right to be a Jew—not by acting like a Gentile but in being himself" (Greenberg, "Jewish Values," 56). Greenberg critiqued the popular melting pot version of American society in which all distinctions melted away and instead saw an opportunity for greater commitment to particular identities. Critiquing a popular movement at the time, Greenberg wrote that "Brotherhood activity in America has been marked by the emphasis on the similar or identical nature of all religions. Implied here is the reason why men are brothers" (Greenberg, "Jewish Values," 56). Rejecting an approach to unity that flattened out differences, Greenberg suggested that "This mode is now being superceded [sic] by a search for a pluralism that respects differences" (Greenberg, "Jewish Values," 56). He discerned that "The will to encounter the other in his own terms opens up the possibility that Judaism can speak in its own authentic categories and yet be heard." (Greenberg, "Jewish Values," 56). In this articulation, Greenberg presented a vision of pluralism that claimed that American Jews could reassert their identity in the context of the changing American ethic and that a Judaism that "can speak in its own authentic categories" should welcome the open society and the opportunity for new encounters.[12] Greenberg recognized an opportunity in the changing American

---

12 It is important to note that Greenberg's commitment to encounter was not only limited to the intra-Jewish, Christian–Jewish, or Jewish–American contexts. His active participation in the delegation of Jews that travelled to Dharamsala, India, in 1990 to engage in dialogue with the Dalai Lama reflected the extent of his commitment to encounter. See Rodger Kamenetz, *The Jew in the Lotus: A Poet's Rediscovery of Jewish Identity in Buddhist India.* (San Francisco: HarperCollins, 1994).

ethic that was hard-wired for diverse encounters. Rather than being a threat to Jewish identity, Greenberg saw it as a goad to strengthening identity in the face of encounter. At the same time, he also perceived the need for a transformation of American Judaism in the form of "new conceptions, techniques and emphases" that would be required to successfully navigate the new American ethic.

The 1960s was an extremely generative decade for Greenberg. His exposure to the historical and theological enormity of the Holocaust in 1961 led him to articulate a vision for a more inclusive American Jewish community and to model that vision through influential intra-Jewish gatherings. It also pushed him to reach out to Christian theologians and work with them to understand the theological legacy of the Holocaust for Christians and Jews. Those two decisions led to Greenberg's evolving identity as a *Klal Yisrael* Jew and a breakthrough in his covenantal theology. Finally, as we have seen in this chapter, Greenberg would explore the meaning of the open society and the increasing reality of cross-group encounters in both practice and in writing. While each of these aspects is essential to Greenberg's theology of Hybrid Judaism, they are incomplete without the final ingredient that provides the theological ground upon which the entire system is built. It is to that final ingredient that we now turn.

# Chapter 9

# The Image of God and Hybrid Judaism

By the end of the 1960s, Greenberg would develop the image of God idea as a validation for Jewish encounters with one another and with the open society. Ultimately, it would provide the theological basis upon which to assert his theology of Hybrid Judaism. Put differently, if the voluntary covenant was the central contribution of Greenberg's covenantal theology, then the image of God idea stands as the orienting concept of his entire theological system. Over the course of the next half century, Greenberg would return again and again to his foundational belief that human beings are created in the image of God. Although the idea has its origins in the Hebrew Bible,[1] Greenberg can be credited with bringing it to the fore in the twentieth century and establishing it as a central meta-value of Judaism.

Returning to Greenberg's 1966 interview in the pages of *The Commentator*, and in addition to the issues raised in Chapter 7, the interview was significant because it was the site of Greenberg's earliest reflections on the image of God idea. In the course of his lengthy answer to the question "What are some contemporary problems to which we could apply *halachic* principles and laws, but don't?" Greenberg cited "the war in Viet Nam and the American attitude toward the welfare of our society" (Goldberg, "Dr. Greenberg," 8).

---

1 Genesis 1:26—"And God said, Let us make man in our image, after our likeness … " and Genesis 5:1—"These are the generations of man. In the day that God created man; in the image of God He made him."

Regarding "the welfare of society," Greenberg drew on classical Jewish sources and opined that

> The central moral principle of the Torah is the belief that man is created in the image of G-d, and this implies that any act or policy which humiliates or 'shrinks' a person is an act of desecration of the Divine image. Belittling man drives the Divine presence out of the world. Thus, Jews are required to eliminate those conditions—physical or psychological—that humiliate people. (Goldberg, "Dr. Greenberg," 8)

Here, Greenberg made the explicit connection between the belief that human beings are created in the image of God and the implications of that belief with regard to the manner in which they are expected to behave. For Greenberg, the theological claim had very practical implications for each and every member of society.

In a lecture delivered at the Wurzweiler School of Social Work at Yeshiva University in 1967,[2] Greenberg revisited the image of God concept. He opened with the question: "What is the fundamental value in Jewish tradition?" (Greenberg, "Jewish Tradition," 1). In his answer, Greenberg turned to a classic Midrashic text[3] that recorded a supposed discussion between Rabbi Akiva and Ben Azzai, scholars of the early second century of the Common Era. To the question of what the fundamental value of the Jewish tradition is, Akiva, somewhat predictably, suggested "Love your neighbor as yourself" (Lev. 19:18). Ben Azzai, however, opted for a less well-known biblical verse: "These are the generations of man. In the day that God created man; in the image of God He made him" (Gen. 5:1). Elaborating on Ben Azzai's selection, Greenberg wrote that "the Talmud draws some of the implications of the concept that man is in the image of God" (Greenberg, "Jewish Tradition," 1). The implications of the text are twofold: one,

---

2  The lecture was later published under the title "Jewish Tradition and Contemporary Problems" in *Relationships Between Jewish and Contemporary Social Issues* (New York: Yeshiva University, 1969): 1–19.

3  *Sifra Kedoshim*, Leviticus 19, 18.

that "each reproduction of the image of God is unique" and, two, that "since man is in the image of God, he has infinite value" [4] (Greenberg, "Jewish Tradition," 1). In light of the dual implications that all human beings are unique and of infinite value, Greenberg echoed his statement in *The Commentator* interview that "there are actions which 'extend' or 'expand' the image of God and there are actions which 'shrink' it … Any act that humiliates, denigrates, or hurts is seen as a form of desecration of the divine image and a reduction of God's presence" (Greenberg, "Jewish Tradition," 2). For Greenberg, the image of God idea established parameters for the way human beings are expected to treat one another.

In 1988, Greenberg and Shalom Freedman would publish a lengthy collection of "conversations" entitled *Living in the Image of God: Jewish Teachings to Perfect the World*. By then, Greenberg's thinking regarding the image of God idea was fully developed and he acknowledged that "The central anchor of my thinking and of my life is the concept that the human being is created in the image of God" (Freedman, *Living in the Image of God*, 31). In its most complete articulation, the image of God idea would ultimately incorporate *three* characteristics. Putting the third and final piece in place, Greenberg described it in this way: "Because humans are in the image of God, they are endowed by their Creator with three intrinsic dignities: infinite value … ; equality … ; and uniqueness. All of society— economics, politics, culture—must be organized to respect and uphold these three fundamental dignities" (Freedman, *Living in the Image of*

---

4  Greenberg's basis for the claims of uniqueness and infinite value are both found in *Mishnah Sanhedrin* 4:5. *Uniqueness:* " … to teach the greatness of the Holy One, Blessed is He: when a man casts many coins from a single mold, they all resemble one another, but the Supreme King of kings, the Holy One, Blessed is He, fashioned each man in the mold of the first man, yet not one of them resembles another." *Infinite value:* "In civil cases, one can make monetary restitution [for judicial errors] and thereby effect his atonement, but in capital cases, he is held responsible for the blood [of the one accused] and the blood of his [potential] descendants until the end of time," and "Man was created alone to teach you that whoever destroys a single life is considered by Scripture as though he destroyed an entire world; and whoever preserves a single life is considered by Scripture as though he had preserved an entire world."

*God,* 31). The complete expression of Greenberg's image of God idea represented a messianic vision for humanity. The call for "all of society" to reorient their collective actions and attain a state in which they would recognize the three intrinsic human dignities of infinite value, equality, and uniqueness represented nothing less than a vision for a perfected world. As such, the implications of the image of God idea for both inter- and intra-group relations would be significant.

In 1997, the *Journal of Ecumenical Studies* published Greenberg's final and most complete treatment of pluralism. As the title suggests, "Seeking the Religious Roots of Pluralism: In the Image of God and Covenant" returned to the two bookends of his theology: the image of God idea and his covenantal theology.[5] Having already considered Greenberg's covenantal theology,[6] I will turn specifically to his idea of the image of God. At the beginning of his essay, Greenberg acknowledged that many religious adherents are suspicious of pluralism.[7] As he put it, some perceived pluralism as "a modern value imposed by cultural pressure on classic religions" (Greenberg, "Seeking the Religious Roots," 385–386). Others saw it as a threat to the absolute claims that religions must make. Yet others raised concerns that "pluralism is correlated with a loss of intensity of religious spirit" and that, as a result, "the mainstream liberal traditions ... are not growing" (Greenberg, "Seeking the Religious Roots," 386).

In responding to these concerns, Greenberg made the case that not only is pluralism defensible, but that "in fact pluralism is grounded in the deep structures of Judaism and of religious life" (Greenberg, "Seeking the Religious Roots," 385–386). Returning to his now familiar trope, Greenberg wrote that "pluralism is grounded in the fundamental principle of Judaism. (Rabbi) Ben Azzai states that the human being as created in the image of God is the *clal gadol*,

---

5  With modernity firmly identified as the beginning of the third era of his covenantal schema, the Holocaust did not receive a single mention by this time and provided no basis for his theological system. See chapter 6, footnote 18.

6  See pp. 86-88.

7  Recall that Greenberg's theology extends beyond pluralism, even as he continued to employ the term.

the central category of Jewish tradition" (Greenberg, "Seeking the Religious Roots," 386). As we have seen, Greenberg's application of the idea that human beings are created in the image of God teaches that they are endowed with three fundamental dignities: infinite value, equality, and uniqueness.

Greenberg went on to explain that, "In the past, these dignities have been obscured by various cultural processes" (Greenberg, "Seeking the Religious Roots," 387). Specifically, Greenberg pointed to "stereotyping" and *"othering"* as the methods by which people used to deny the image of God that inheres within all people. He continued that, "In the past, most value systems (including religion and culture) created and functionally transmitted their values by establishing an inside group ... its own values and its own religious claims were superior" (Greenberg, "Seeking the Religious Roots," 387). Therefore, as a result of this "inside/outside dichotomy ... The outsiders were inferior, of little or no value." This view "was reinforced by the cultural stereotypes that naturally follow when you begin with the assumption of insider superiority and sustain it by having little contact with others" (Greenberg, "Seeking the Religious Roots," 387). Here, the crucial point comes into focus: separation facilitates the kind of "stereotyping" and *"othering"* that Greenberg saw as a barrier to realizing the full (i.e., infinite) value of one another. As such, the solution to the denial of the image of God was clear: images of God must encounter one another.

For Greenberg, the period that began with the European Enlightenment and Emancipation—modernity—represented the greatest opportunity for human encounter yet. Contrasting past encounters between members of different religions in which one religious group would often have to succumb to the other (or choose the alternatives of death or exile), Greenberg observed that "In the modern condition, coming to know the other faith frequently occurs without the conquest of one's own ... religion" (Greenberg, "Seeking the Religious Roots," 388). Instead, "Modern culture made an initial sociological contribution to the growth of pluralism and the undermining of absolute (superiority) claims.

Modern culture differentially created urban settings where everybody mixes. There the other is encountered, not as a stranger … " (Greenberg, "Seeking the Religious Roots," 387). As a result, "Pluralism is the natural outgrowth of this experience. First comes the encounter, followed by the recognition and then by affirmation of the uniqueness and equality of the other" (Greenberg, "Seeking the Religious Roots," 388).[8] The newfound ability to have contact with one another without the fear of suppression meant that human beings could fully recognize the image of God in each other. The modern opportunity for encounter—more present in the contemporary United States than possibly at any other time or place in history—resulted in a situation that "has evoked a recognition of the other as no longer other but as the image of God" (Greenberg, "Seeking the Religious Roots," 388). Crucially, for Greenberg, the impact of these encounters would not end with the realization of the uniqueness, equality, and infinite value of the other. They would also result in a recognition of the other that would be transformative.

Having established the theological importance of encounter as a path to realizing the image of God in each other, Greenberg made his most far-reaching claim:

> The result [of encounter] is the coexistence in the believer's mind and experience of two (or more) religious systems whose claims and expressions are experienced as vitally (perhaps, equally) alive and valid. This gives rise to the plurality of affirmations. (Greenberg, "Seeking the Religious Roots," 388)

The importance of this claim cannot be overstated. Greenberg was clear in his interpretation of the potential power of encounter. A religionist, as a direct result of one's full encounter with, and

---

8 Even at this late stage in his thinking, Greenberg continued to use the misnomer "pluralism."

recognition of, another person's inherent value as an image of God, could potentially come to appreciate that person's faith as an equally valid and valuable religious system and, as a result, affirm the truth of that faith in addition to one's own.[9] The result is nothing short of a postethnic understanding of religious identity.[10]

Lest the reader conclude that this was an errant phrase in one of Greenberg's many publications, it is worthwhile to offer additional evidence. In a short piece that was published in the pages of the journal Sh'ma in 1999, Greenberg returned to the theme of encounter and reasserted his point, this time even more clearly. In his submission, entitled "The Principles of Pluralism," Greenberg wrote that,

> In appreciation of an open society and of the equality and uniqueness of others, I come to affirm the value of living and of teaching in the presence of other truths and systems. Other approaches teach me the limitations of my own views—preventing an imperialist extension of my truth/faith beyond its legitimate sphere into realms where it becomes a lie or is wrongly applied. And while I may come to refute or reject some contradictories, I may also learn from others' insights and may even integrate them,

---

9 Greenberg never explicitly makes the jump from the affirmation of the validity of another religion to the realm of practice—that is, asserting that after discovering the validity of a given ritual in another faith, one should adopt it; however, the possibility of such a transformation is implicit in the system.

10 In "Religious Roots," Greenberg proceeded to distinguish this from "relativism," which he described as "the conclusion ... that all claimed truths are equally true or untrue." Instead, Greenberg claimed that pluralism "leaves room to say 'no' to other religious faiths and moral value systems. Pluralism does not mean that there cannot be genuine disagreement and conflict between faiths. Pluralism does not rule out as legitimate the conviction that the other faith system incorporates serious errors or mistakes. Pluralism includes the possibility that some value systems and some religious systems are indeed not legitimate; therefore, they should not be legitimated within the framework of pluralism" (Greenberg, "Seeking the Religious Roots," 389). Of course, the fact that his understanding of pluralism allows for the *affirmation* of some "value systems and religious systems" is the innovation in his theology.

thus improving my own system. (Greenberg, "Principles of Pluralism," 5)

Here, again, Greenberg extended the image of God idea ("equality and uniqueness") to affirm the adoption of ideas from other systems as a way of improving one's own. It is in this statement that Greenberg presented the fullness of his theology of religious encounter as one that can result in transformation.[11]

To be sure, this claim raises important questions: to what extent can one adopt the "insights" of other systems? What will become of Judaism if it is transformed in the process of encounter and transformation? Are there/should there be any limits? Throughout his career, Greenberg was clear that "the tradition ha[s] the capacity to cope with the toughest questions" (Butler and Nagel, *My Yeshiva College*, 180) and that "If [Judaism] is divine, surely it can outlast the wreckage of an earlier ethos" (Greenberg, "Jewish Values," 52). Although, despite his confidence in the ability of Judaism to withstand the transformative power of modernity, he was also open to other possibilities. As he has acknowledged, "the transformation as a result of encounter has no guarantees" and that while "selfishly, if someone 'left' it would be a greater loss to the Jewish people, ultimately, as long as they are covenant-minded, it is OK" (Greenberg,

---

11  Here, I am in disagreement with Sandra Lubarsky's claim that

> for Greenberg, religious pluralism calls on individuals to clarify their faith commitments and to choose one tradition over another. He does not address the possibility that pluralism may result in new forms of traditions. Intermarriage and the identity issue raised by the emergence of hybrid religious identities (such as Jewish-Buddhists) have not been addressed as issues related to religious pluralism. Both issues challenge the essentialism of traditions in a direct way, clearly violating boundaries ... thus far, Jewish thinking about religious pluralism has assumed boundaried entities. (Lubarsky, "Deep Religious Pluralism," 128)

In fact, and as I have shown throughout Part II, Greenberg's theology of religious pluralism does precisely what Lubarsky has called for; he is acutely aware of the "identity issue" and is anything but essentialist, or concerned about "violating boundaries." Lubarsky's citations reveal that she based her conclusions on a small selection of Greenberg's writings that prevented her from seeing the full unfolding of his theology.

Yarnton Interview, 2014).[12] For Greenberg, the covenantal partnership between humanity and the divine in the realization of redemption is more important than the particular claims of a given religious community. It was no understatement when he wrote that "in our era of pluralism, we are living in an age of great religious breakthroughs" (Greenberg, "Seeking the Religious Roots," 394).

As is now clear, Irving Greenberg's theological system is mistakenly described (by himself and others) as a theology of religious pluralism. His understanding of pluralism is radically different from Horace Kallen's articulation of cultural pluralism. In Kallen's early-twentieth-century sociological model, the United States was described as a diverse country made up of a wide range of distinct ethnic groups. What made American democracy so powerful, according to Kallen, was that it allowed for these different groups to live side by side without having to abandon their identities to a melting pot of homogeneity. By comparing America to an orchestra, Kallen imagined that each of these ethnic groups would retain its own identity and remain distinct from the other groups, even as it participated in the symphony of American democracy. In his conceptualization of cultural pluralism, Kallen failed to account for the impact of social mixing among the different ethnic groups.

By contrast, and shifting from Kallen's focus on ethnicity to the realm of religion, Greenberg's theology of religious pluralism is based on the assumption that, in an open society, people will necessarily interact with each other as equals. His willingness to accept the implications of such encounters locates him not in the pluralist camp, but rather at the very cutting edge of postethnic thinking. As such, Greenberg's system is better described in postethnic terms as a theology of encounter that I call Hybrid Judaism.

---

12 This quote is taken from an interview between the author and Greenberg while both were attending the Oxford Summer Institute in Modern and Contemporary Judaism, in the summer of 2014. The Institute addressed the topic of "Modern Orthodoxy and the Road Not Taken: A Critical Exploration of Questions Arising from the Thought of Rabbi Dr. Irving 'Yitz' Greenberg."

The term "Hybrid Judaism" fuses the multiple with the singular. The sense in which I employ the term hybrid is intended to refer to "Anything derived from heterogeneous sources, or composed of different or incongruous elements" (*OED*). By linking Judaism to hybridity, I am indicating Greenberg's preference for a primary, rooted, group identity (= Jewish) while acknowledging that, in a postethnic reality, one is attached to, and influenced by, more than any one single identity group. To echo David Hollinger, Irving Greenberg's theology of Hybrid Judaism would not have "appealed to Horace Kallen."

By way of summary, it is useful at this point to return to David Hollinger's conception of postethnicity to fully appreciate the parallels with Greenberg's theology of Hybrid Judaism. Hollinger described postethnicity in this way:

> Postethnicity prefers voluntary to prescribed affiliations, appreciates multiple identities, pushes for communities of wide scope ... and accepts the formation of new groups as a part of the normal life of a democratic society. (Hollinger, *Postethnic America*, 116)

Greenberg's perspective with regard to religious groups anticipated much of Hollinger's postethnic framework. Like Hollinger's postethnic preference for voluntary affiliations, Greenberg's covenantal theology identified the modern era as one in which Jews are free to choose whether and how to participate in the voluntary covenant. The postethnic appreciation for multiple, overlapping identities also has resonance with Greenberg's theology. As we have seen, Greenberg's image of God–based conception of pluralism welcomed what he has referred to as "a plurality of affirmations." While Greenberg would prefer that Jews remain rooted in Judaism and the Jewish community, he acknowledged that a commitment to encounter must recognize the possibility that Jews could adopt the truths of more than one religious community. Subsequently, as religionists begin to integrate insights (and practices, to be sure) from other denominations or religions, the lines dividing one identity group from another become porous.

The postethnic push "for communities of wide scope" is parallel to Greenberg's eager willingness to engage the open society and enter into dialogue with non-Orthodox Jews and non-Jews alike, the results of which are now clear to see. Finally, the postethnic acceptance of the formation of new groups is built in to Greenberg's covenantal theology. If, in the third stage of the covenant, Jews are no longer commanded, then any expression of Judaism that affirms the three fundamental dignities inherent in the image of God idea is theologically valid. Taken together, these are the full implications of Greenberg's transformative theology of encounter that I call Hybrid Judaism.

# Conclusion

American Judaism is Hybrid Judaism. The postethnic reality that David Hollinger has described is as prevalent, if not more so, in the American Jewish context as in any other. As Shaul Magid has described it, "[American] Judaism [exists] in an increasingly postethnic world, a world where identities are mixed, where allegiances are more voluntary than inherited, more the result of consent than descent" (Magid, *American Post-Judaism*, 5). Just as lived religion in America is more diverse and complex than it was once imagined to be, the same is true for American Judaism. As a result, pluralism, as both a descriptive tool and a prescriptive approach, is no longer adequate to help navigate the contemporary American Jewish landscape. We need new ways of understanding and responding to the American Jewish community that are sensitive to the transformative role of encounter. David Hollinger's conception of postethnicity and Irving Greenberg's theology of Hybrid Judaism have provided us with just such understandings.

Irving Greenberg's theology of hybrid Judaism presents a vision for the future of the American Jewish community in particular, and humanity in general, that is both disruptive and redemptive at the same time. Disruptive, because it imagines—and welcomes—a present and future in which identity is fluid and potentially changing at any time. In a reality in which each person encounters the other as an image of God, one's grandparents have very little hold on the identity of their grandchildren, even if one acknowledges, with Kallen, that they cannot be changed. Redemptive, because it imagines a world in which human beings recognize in each other the fundamental dignities of an image of God—infinite value, equality, and uniqueness—and, as a result, open themselves up to encountering each other in transformative ways. As a result, individual identity becomes a patchwork quilt, stitched together by a multitude of materials that represent the "several we's of which the individual is a part" (Hollinger, *Postethnic America*, 106).

Taken together, Hollinger and Greenberg, respectively, present a sociological framework for understanding, and a theological basis for embracing, the changing nature of American Jewish identity. To be sure, for many, these ideas will represent a step too far. For others, there will be the realization that much of what I have written is simply descriptive of the reality around them. In truth, what Hollinger has described in sociological terms and Greenberg has validated in the language of theology, is more the norm than the exception when it comes to the contemporary American Jewish community. Of course, this does not mean that everyone has to embrace the reality I have described. But, if they are to understand some of what is taking place in the American Jewish community, they will do well to at least pay attention to what I have outlined.

The subject of Hybrid Judaism encourages us to rethink our understanding of our American Jewish reality. In the era of hybrid Judaism, I suggest that we move the conversation from one about individual identity and status—that is, membership and notions of Jewish Peoplehood—and focus instead on Jewish communities, *in all their diversity*. When the focus is shifted from questions of individual status to those of community affiliation, we realize that anyone can participate (of course, some communities will still exclude individuals that fail to meet their standards). A recognition of the increasingly hybrid nature of American Jewish identity should lead us to the recognition that what matters is whether people wish to be affiliated with the Jewish community, not how, or to what extent, they choose to identify themselves. As a result, our Jewish communities will grow, even as their constitution will likely undergo significant change. The result will be a Jewish community that, rather than remaining self-absorbed with its own survival, can turn its focus to the perfection of humanity through transformative encounters.

# Bibliography

"A Portrait of American Jewish Americans." Pew Research Center, Washington, DC, October 1, 2013. Accessed July 24, 2016. http://www.pewforum.org/2013/10/01/jewish-american-beliefs-attitudes-culture-survey/

"America's Changing Religious Landscape." Pew Research Center, Washington, DC, May 12, 2015. Accessed July 24, 2016. http://www.pewforum.org/2015/05/12/new-pew-research-center-study-examines-americas-changing-religious-landscape/

"Rabbi Answers Zangwill." *The New York Times*, November 16, 1908.

"3 Branches of Judaism Meet in Effort to Improve Ties." *The New York Times*, June 23, 1969: 41.

Ahlstrom, Sydney E. *A Religious History of the American People.* New Haven: Yale University Press, 1972.

Albanese, Catherine L. *America: Religion and Religions*, 3rd ed. Belmont: Wadsworth Publishing Company, 1999.

———. *American Religious History: A Bibliographical Essay.* Washington, DC: United States Department of State, 2002.

Baird, Robert. *Religion in America, or, An account of the origin, progress, relation to the state, and present condition of the evangelical churches in the United States: with notices of the unevangelical denomenations.* New York: Harper & Brothers, 1844.

Ben Hamon. "The Reform Rabbis Debate Theology." *Judaism* 12, no. 4 (1963): 479–486.

Bender, Courtney and Pamela E. Klassen, eds. *After Pluralism: Reimagining Religious Engagement.* New York: Columbia University Press, 2010.

Beneke, Chris. *Beyond Toleration: The Religious Origins of American Pluralism.* Oxford: Oxford University Press, 2006.

Berger, Peter L. *The Heretical Imperative: Contemporary Possibilities of Religious Affirmation*. Garden City: Anchor Press/Doubleday, 1979.

Berman, Lila Corwin. *Speaking of Jews: Rabbis, Intellectuals, and the Creation of an American Public Identity*. Berkeley: University of California Press, 2009.

Bhabha, Homi K. *The Location of Culture*. New York: Routledge, 1994.

Biale, David. "The Melting Pot and Beyond: Jews and the Politics of American Identity." In *Insider/Outsider: American Jews and Multiculturalism*, edited by David Biale, Michael Galchinsky, and Sussanah Heschel, 17–33. Berkeley: University of Califorina Press, 1998.

Bokser, Ben Zion. *Abraham Isaac Kook: The Lights of Penitence, Lights of Holiness, The Moral Principles, Essays, Letters, and Poems*. Mahwah: Paulist Press, 1978.

Boris, Staci. "The New Authentics: Artists of the Post-Jewish Generation." In *The New Authentics: Artists of the Post-Jewish Generation*, 19–43. Chicago: Spertus Press, 2007.

Brauer, Jerald C. *Reinterpretation in American Church History*. Chicago: The University of Chicago Press, 1968.

Bristow, Edward, ed. *No Religion is an Island: The Nostra Aetate Dialogues*. New York: Fordham University Press, 1998.

Brook, Vincent, ed. *You Should See Yourself: Jewish Identity in Postmodern American Culture*. New Brunswick: Rutgers University Press, 2006.

Brown, Wendy. *Regulating Aversion: Tolerance in the Age of Identity and Empire*. Princeton: Princeton University Press, 2006.

Butler, Menachem and Zev Nagel, eds. *My Yeshiva College: 75 Years of Memories*. Yashar Books, 2006.

Cesarani, David and Eric J. Sundquist, eds. *After the Holocaust: Challenging the Myth of Silence*. New York: Routledge, 2012.

Cohen, Charles L. and Ronald L. Numbers, eds. *Gods in America: Religious Pluralism in the United Staes*. Oxford: Oxford University Press, 2013.

Cohen, Shaye J. D. *From the Maccabees to the Mishnah*, 2nd ed. Louisville: Westminster John Knox Press, 2006.

Cohen, Stuart, and Bernard Susser, eds. *Ambivalent Jew: Charles Liebman in Memoriam*. New York: The Jewish Theological Seminary of America, 2007.

Connolly, William E. *Pluralism*. Durham: Duke University Press, 2005.

Cooper, Simon. *Contemporary Covenantal Thought: Interpretations of Covenant in the Thought of David Hartman and Eugene Borowitz*. Boston: Academic Studies Press, 2012.

Cooperman, Jessica. "'A Little Army Discipline Would Improve the Whole House of Israel': The Jewish Welfare Board, State Power and the Shaping of Jewish Identity in World War I America." PhD diss., New York University, 2010.

Diner, Hasia. *The Jews of the United States*. Berkeley: University of California Press, 2004.

———. "Like the Antelope and the Badger: The Founding and Early Years of JTS, 1886–1902." In *Tradition Renewed: A History of the Jewish Theological Seminary of America*, edited by Jack Wertheimer, 3–42. New York: The Jewish Theological Seminary of America, 1997.

———. *We Remember with Reverence and Love: American Jews and the Myth of Silence after the Holocaust, 1945–1962*. New York: New York University Press, 2009.

Fackenheim, Emil L. *God's Presence in History: Jewish Affirmations and Philosophical Reflections*. New York: Harper & Row, 1970.

Ferziger, Adam S. *Beyond Sectarianism: The Realignment of American Orthodox Judaism*. Detroit: Wayne State University Press, 2015.

———. "Church/Sect Theory and American Orthodoxy Reconsidered." In *Ambivalent Jew: Charles Liebman in Memorium*, edited by Stuart Cohen and Bernard Susser, 107–123. New York: The Jewish Theological Seminary of America, 2007.

Fessenden, Tracy. "Race." In *Themes in Religions and American Culture*, edited by Philip Goff and Paul Harvey, 129–161. Chapel Hill: The University of North Carolina Press, 2004.

Fisher, Eugene J., James A. Rudin, and Marc H. Tanenbaum, eds. *Twenty Years of Jewish-Catholic Relations*. New York: Paulist Press, 1986.

Fiske, Edward B. "Jewish Theologians Are Reviving an Increase in the Recovery of Traditonal Customs and Teachings." *The New York Times*, November 23, 1969: 65.

———. "Rethinking by Jews." *The New York Times*, May 21, 1967: E4.

Fleischner, Eva, ed. *Auschwitz: Beginning of a New Era? Reflections on the World.* New York: KTAV, 1977.

Freedman, Shalom. *Living in the Image of God: Jewish Teachings to Perfect the World.* Lanham: Rowman & Littlefield Publishers, Inc., 1998.

Frymer-Kensky, Tikva, David Novak, Peter Ochs, David Fox Sandmel, and Michael A. Signer, eds. *Christianity in Jewish Terms.* Boulder: Westview Press, 2000.

Gaustad, Edwin, and Leigh Schmidt. *The Religious History of America: The Heart of the American Story from Colonial Times to Today.* New York: Harper One, 2002.

Glazer, Nathan. *We Are All Multiculturalists Now.* Cambridge: Harvard University Press, 1997.

Glazer, Nathan, and Daniel Patrick Moynihan. *Beyond the Melting Pot: The Negroes, Puerto Ricans, Jews, Italians, and Irish of New York City,* 2nd ed. Cambridge: MIT Press, 1970.

Gleason, Philip. "Review of Postethnic America: Beyond Multiculturalism." *The Journal of American History* 84, no. 4 (1996): 1658–1659.

Goff, Philip, and Paul Harvey. *Themes in Religion & American Culture.* Chapel Hill: The University of North Carolina Press, 2004.

Goldberg, Harold. "Dr. Greenberg Discusses Orthodoxy, YU, Viet Nam, & Sex." *The Commentator,* April 28, 1966: 6, 8–10.

———. "Rejoinder." *Jewish Action,* Winter 5751/1990–91, 29–34.

Golden, Jonathan J. "From Cooperation to Confrontation: The Rise and Fall of the Synagogue Council of America." PhD diss., Brandeis University, 2008.

Gordon, Milton M. *Assimilation in American Life: The Role of Race, Religion, and National Origins.* New York: Oxford University Press, 1964.

Greenberg, Irving. "Adventure in Freedom—Or Escape From Freedom?: Jewish Identity in America." *American Jewish Historical Quarterly* 55, no. 1 (1965): 5–21.

———. "Book Review—Assimilation in American Life: The Role of Race, Religious and National Origins. By Milton M. Gordon." *American Jewish Historical Quarterly* 55, no. 3 (1966): 391–393.

———. "Cloud of Smoke, Pillar of Fire: Judaisms, Christianity, and Modernity after the Holocaust." In *Auschwitz: Beginning of a New Era?*, edited by Eva Fleischner, 7–55. Jersey City: KTAV Publishing House, Inc., 1977.

———. "The End of Emancipation." *Conservative Judaism* 30, no. 4 (1976): 47–63.

———. *For the Sake of Heaven and Earth: The New Encounter Between Judaism and Christianity.* Philadelpia: The Jewish Publication Society, 2004.

———. "Greenberg Clarifies and Defends his Views." *The Commentator*, May 12, 1966: 8-9.

———. "Jewish Tradition and Contemporary Problems." In *Relationships Between Jewish and Contemporary Social Issues.* New York: Yeshiva University, 1969. 1–19.

———. "Jewish Values and the Changing American Ethic." *Tradition: A Journal of Orthodox Thought* 10, no. 1 (1968): 42–74.

———. "A Lifetime of Encounter with the Rav." *The Commentator.* March 26, 2007.

———. "The New Encounter of Judaism and Chrisitianity." *Barat Review* 3, no. 2 (1967): 113–125.

———. "On the Relationship of Jews and Christians and of Jews and Jews." *Jewish Action*, Winter 5751/1990–91, 20, 22-24, 26, 28.

———. "The Principles of Pluralism." *Sh'ma* 29, no. 561 (1999): 4–5.

———. "The Relationship of Judaism and Christianity: Toward a New Organic Model." In *Twenty Years of Jewish-Catholic Relations*, edited by Eugene J. Fisher, A. James Rudin, and Marc H. Tanenbaum, 191–211. New York: Paulist Press, 1986.

———. "Seeking the Religious Roots of Pluralism: In the Image of God and Covenant." *Journal of Ecumenical Studies* 34, no. 3 (1997): 385–394.

———. *Theodore Roosevelt and Labor: 1900-1918.* New York: Garland Publishing, Inc., 1988.

———. "Theology after the Shoah: The Transformation of the Core Paradigm." *Modern Judaism* 26, no. 3 (2006): 213–239.

———. "The Third Great Cycle of Jewish History." *Perspectives*, 1981: 1–26.

———. "Towards a Principled Pluralism." *Perspectives*, 1986: 20–31.

———. "Voluntary Covenant." *Perspectives*, 1982: 27–44.

———. "Will there be One Jewish People by the Year 2000?" *Perspectives*, 1986: 1–8.

———. "Yavneh: Looking Ahead, Values and Goals." *Yavneh Studies: A Jewish Collegiate Publication* 1, no.1 (1962): 47-49.

Greenberg, Irving, Mordecai M. Kaplan, Jakob J. Petuchowski, and Seymour Siegel. "Toward Jewish Religious Unity: A Symposium." *Judaism* 15, no. 2 (1966): 129–163.

Greene, Daniel. *The Jewish Origins of Cultural Pluralism: The Menorah Association and American Diversity.* Bloomington: Indiana University Press, 2011.

Gurock, Jeffrey S., and Jacob J. Schacter. *A Modern Heretic and a Traditional Community: Mordecai M. Kaplan, Orthodoxy, and American Judaism.* New York: Columbia University Press, 1997.

Hackett, David G. *Religion and American Culture.* New York: Routledge, 1995.

Heilman, Samuel C. *Sliding to the Right: The Contest for the Future of American Jewish Orthodoxy.* Berkeley: University of California Press, 2006.

Herberg, Will. *Judaism and Modern Man: An Interpretation of Jewish Religion.* Woodstock: Jewish Lights Publishing, 1997.

———. *Protestant-Catholic-Jew: An Essay in American Religous Sociology.* Chicago: The University of Chicago Press, 1983 (reprint of 1955 original publication).

Hollinger, David A. *Postethnic America: Beyond Multiculturalism.* New York: Basic Books, 2005.

Horowitz, C. Morris, and Lawrence Kaplan. *The Jewish Population of the New York Area, 1900–1975.* New York: Federation of Jewish Philanthropies of New York, 1959.

Hutchison, William R. *Religious Pluralism in America: The Contentious History of a Founding Ideal.* New Haven: Yale University Press, 2003.

Jaffee, Martin S. *The End of Jewish Radar: Snapshots of a Postethnic American Judaism.* New York: iUniverse, Inc., 2009.

Jakobsen, Janet R. "Ethics After Pluralism." In *After Pluralism: Reimagining Religious Engagement*, edited by Courtney Bender and Janet R. Jakobsen, 31–58. New York: Columbia University Press, 2010.

James, William. *A Pluralistic Universe.* New York: Longmans, Green & Co., 1909.

Kallen, Horace M. *Culture and Democracy in the United States.* New Brunswick, NJ: Transaction Publishers, 1998 (originally published in 1924).

———. "Democracy versus the Melting-Pot: A Study of American Nationality: Part I," *The Nation,* February 18, 1915: 190–194.

———. "Democracy versus the Melting-Pot: A Study of American Nationality: Part II," *The Nation,* February 25, 1915: 217–220.

———. "The Ethics of Zionism." *Maccabean* 11, no. 2 (1906): 61–71.

———. "Nationality and the Hyphenated American." *The Menorah Journal* I, no. 2 (Apr. 1915): 79–86.

Kamenetz, Rodger. *The Jew in the Lotus: A Poet's Rediscovery of Jewish Identity in Buddhist India.* New York: HarperCollins, 1994.

Kaplan, Mordecai M. *Judaism as a Civilization: Toward a Reconstruction of American-Jewish Life.* New York: Schocken Books, 1972 (originally published in 1934).

Katkin, Wendy F., Ned Landsman, and Andrea Tyree, eds. *Beyond Pluralism: The Conception of Groups and Group Identities in America.* Urbana: University of Illinois Press, 1998.

Katz, Steven T. *Historicism, the Holocaust, and Zionism: Critical Studies in Modern Jewish Thought and History.* New York: New York University Press, 1992.

———. "Irving (Yitzchak) Greenberg." In *Interpretations of Judaism in the Late Twentieth Century,* edited by Steven T. Katz, 59–89. Washington, DC: B'nai B'rith Books, 1993.

Katz, Steven T. and Steven Bayme, eds. *Continuity and Change: A Festschrift in Honor of Irving Greenberg's 75th Birthday.* Lanham: University Press of America, Inc., 2010.

Katz, Steven T., Shlomo Biderman, and Gershon Greenberg. *Wrestling with God: Jewish Theological Responses during and after the Holocaust.* Oxford: Oxford University Press, 2007.

Kay, Michael Aaron. "The Paradox of Pluralism: Leadership and Community Building in Pluralistic Jewish High Schools." PhD diss., New York University, 2009.

Kennedy, Ruby Jo Reeves. "Single or Triple Melting Pot? Intermarriage Trends in New Haven, 1870–1940." *American Journal of Sociology* 49, no. 4 (1944): 331–339.

Kozinski, Thaddeus J. *The Political Problem of Pluralism: And Why Philosphers Can't Solve It.* Lanham: Lexington Books, 2010.

Kraut, Benny. *The Greening of American Orthodoxy: Yanveh in the Nineteen Sixties.* Cincinnati: Hebrew Union College Press, 2011.

Krell, Marc A. *Intersecting Pathways: Modern Jewish Theologians in Conversation with Christianity.* Oxford: Oxford University Press, 2003.

Kronish, Ronald. "John Dewey and Horace M. Kallen on Cultural Pluralism: Their Impact on Jewish Education." *Jewish Social Studies* 44, no. 2 (1982): 135–148.

Lichtenstein, Aharon. "Rav Lichtenstein Writes Letter to Dr. Greenberg/Rav Lichtenstein Answers Dr. Greenberg's Article." *The Commentator,* June 2, 1966: 7–8.

Liebman, Charles S., "A Sociological Analysis of Contemporary Orthodoxy," *Judaism* 13, no. 3 (1964): 285–304.

Linenthal, Edward T. *Preserving Memory: The Struggle to Create America's Holocaust Museum.* New York: Columbia University Press, 2001.

Locke, Alain, and Bernhard J. Stern. *When Peoples Meet: A Study in Race and Culture Contacts.* New York: Hinds, Hayden & Eldredge, Inc., 1946.

Lubarsky, Sandra B. "Deep Religious Pluralism and Contemporary Jewish Thought." In *Deep Religious Pluralism,* edited by David Ray Griffin, 111–129. Louisville: Westminster John Knox Press, 2005.

MacHacek, David W. "The Problem of Pluralism." *Sociology of Religion* 64, no. 2 (2003): 145–161.

Magid, Shaul. *American Post-Judaism: Identity and Renewal in a Postethnic Society.* Bloomington: Indiana University Press, 2013.

Marom, Daniel. "Who's Afraid of Horace Kallen? Cultural Pluralism and Jewish Education." *Studies in Jewish Education* 13 (2009): 283–337.

Marsden, George. *Religion and American Culture.* Belmont: Wadsworth, 2001.

Masuzawa, Tomoko. *The Invention of World Religions or, How European Universalism Was Preserved in the Language of Pluralism.* Chicago: The University of Chicago Press, 2005.

Mead, Sidney E. "By Puritans Possessed." *Worldview* 16, no. 4 (1973): 49–52.

Michaelson, Robert S. "Red Man's Religion/White Man's Religious History." *Journal of the American Academy of Religion* 51, no. 4 (1983): 667–684.

Monsoma, Stephen V., and J. Christopher Soper. *The Challenge of Pluralism: Church and State in Five Democracies.* Lanham: Rowman & Littlefield Publishers, Inc., 2009.

Montgomery, Paul L. "A Dialogue of Faiths at Seton Hall." *The New York Times,* October 29, 1970: 45.

Moore, Deborah Dash. *B'nai B'rith and the Challenge of Ethnic Leadership.* Albany: State University of New York Press, 1981.

Moore, R. Laurence. *Religious Outsiders and the Making of Americans.* New York: Oxford University Press, 1986.

Morgan, Michael L. *Beyond Auschwitz: Post-Holocaust Jewish Thought in America.* Oxford: Oxford University Press, 2001.

Newman, William M. *American Pluralism: A Study of Minority Groups and Social Theory.* Harper & Row, 1973.

Novak, Michael. *Unmeltable Ethnics: Politics & Culture in American Life.* New York: Macmillan Publishing Company, 1972.

Oppenheim, Michael. "Irving Greenberg and a Jewish Dialectic of Hope." *Judaism: A Quarterly Journal of Jewish Life and Thought* 49, no. 194 (2000): 189–203.

Orsi, Robert A., George Marsden, David W. Wills, and Colleen McDannell. "The Decade Ahead in Scholarship." *Religion in American Culture: A Journal of Interpretation* 3, no. 1 (1993): 1–28.

*Oxford English Dictionary,* s.v. "hybrid, n. and adj." Accessed July 31, 2016. http://www.oed.com.ezproxy.stanford.edu/view/Entry/89809?redirectedFrom=hybrid&

———. s.v. "pluralism, n." Accessed July 31, 2016. http://www.oed.com.ezproxy.stanford.edu/view/Entry/146193?redirectedFrom=pluralism#eid

Parnes, Stephan O., ed. *Prayer Book: For the Jewish Personnel in the Armed Forces of the United States.* Washington, DC: Commission on Jewish Chaplaincy of JWB, 1984.

Pianko, Noam. *Jewish Peoplehood: An American Innovation.* New Brunswick: Rutgers University Press, 2015.

————. "'The True Liberalism of Zionism': Horace Kallen, Jewish Nationalism, and the Limits of American Pluralism." *American Jewish History* 94, no. 4 (2008): 299–329.

Portnoff, Sharon, James A. Diamond, and Martin D. Yaffe, eds. *Emil L. Fackenheim: Philosopher, Theologian, Jew.* Leiden, The Netherlands: Brill, 2008.

Putnam, Robert D., and David E. Campbell. *American Grace: How Religion Divides and Unites Us.* New York: Simon & Schuster, 2010.

Rosman, Moshe. *How Jewish is Jewish History?* Oxford: Littman Library of Jewish Civilization, 2007.

Sarna, Jonathan D. *American Judaism: A History.* New Haven: Yale University Press, 2004.

————. *Minority Faiths and the American Protestant Mainstream.* Champaign: University of Illinois Press, 1998.

————. "The Relationship of Orthodox Jews with Believing Jews of Other Religious Ideologies and Non-Believing Jews: The American Situation in Historical Perspective." In *The Relationship of Orthodox Jews with Believing Jews of Other Religious Ideologies and Non-Believing Jews,* by Adam Mintz, 1–26. New York: Yeshiva University Press, 2010.

Schaff, Philip. *America: A Sketch of the Political, Social, and Religious Character of the United States of North America, in Two Lectures, Delivered at Berlin, with a report read before the German Church Diet at Frankfort-on-the-Maine, Sept., 1854.* New York: C. Scribner, 1855.

Schultz, Kevin M. "Protestant-Catholic-Jew, Then and Now." *First Things,* January 2006. Accessed July 23, 2016. http://www.firstthings.com/article/2006/01/protestant-catholic-jewthen-and-now

————. *Tri-Faith America: How Catholics and Jews Held Postwar America to Its Protestant Promise.* New York: Oxford University Press, 2011.

Schultz, Kevin M., and Paul Harvey. "Everywhere and Nowhere: Recent Trends in American Religious History and Historiography." *Journal of the American Academy of Religion* 78, no. 1 (2010): 129–162.

Scult, Mel. *Communings of the Spirit: The Journals of Mordecai M. Kaplan, Volume I, 1913–1934.* Detroit: Wayne State University Press, 2001.

Shapiro, Edward. "Will Herberg's Protestant-Catholic-Jew: A Critique." In *Key Texts in American Jewish Culture*, edited by Jack Kugelmass, 258–274. New Brunswick: Rutgers University Press, 2003.

Singer, David. "Debating Modern Orthodoxy at Yeshiva College: The Greenberg-Lichtenstein Exchange of 1966." *Modern Judaism* 26, no. 2 (2006): 113–126.

Sklare, Marshall. "Discussant." *American Jewish Historical Quarterly* 55, no. 1 (1965): 32–36.

Sollors, Werner. *Beyond Ethnicity: Consent and Descent in American Culture.* New York: Oxford University Press, 1986.

———. "A Critique of Pure Pluralism." In *Reconstructing American Literary History*, edited by Sacvan Bercovitch, 250–279. Cambridge: Harvard University Press, 1986.

———. "Rev. of Postethnic America: Beyond Multiculturalism." *The American Historical Review* 102, no. 2 (1997): 570–571.

Soloveitchik, Joseph B. "Confrontation." *Tradition: A Journal of Orthodox Jewish Thought* 6, no. 2 (1964): 5–29.

———. *Fate and Destiny: From the Holocaust to the State of Israel.* Hoboken: KTAV, 2000.

Turetsky, Yehuda, and Chaim I. Waxman. "Sliding to the Left?: Contemporary American Modern Orthodoxy." *Modern Judaism* 31, no. 2 (2011): 119–141.

Tweed, Thomas A. *Retelling U.S. Religious History.* Berkeley: University of Califorina Press, 1997.

Waters, Mary C. "Multiple Ethnic Identity Choices." In *Beyond Pluralism: The Conception of Groups and Group Identities in America*, edited by Wendy F. Katkin, Ned Landsman, and Andrea Tyree, 28–46.

Wertheimer, Jack. "Recent Trends in American Judaism." *American Jewish Yearbook.* Scranton: American Jewish Committee (AJC), 1989: 63–162.

Young, Robert J. C. *Colonial Desire: Hybridity in Theory, Culture, and Race.* New York: Routledge, 1995.

Zangwill, Israel. *The Melting Pot. A Drama in Four Acts.* New York: Macmillan, 1909.

# Index

CPSIA information can be obtained
at www.ICGtesting.com
Printed in the USA
FSOW03n1055241216
28563FS